WEDDING TRADITIONS

WEDDING TRADITIONS
HERE COMES THE BRIDE

JOANNE DUBBS BALL & CAROLINE TOREM-CRAIG

ANTIQUE TRADER BOOKS
A division of Landmark Specialty Publications

ISBN: 0-930625-63-3
Library of Congress Catalog Card Number: 97-72681

Editor: *Kyle Husfloen*
Editorial Assistant: *Elizabeth Stephan*
Designer: *Jaro Sebek*
Cover Design: *Jaro Sebek*

Cover photo credits:
Front cover: Postcard based on "The Wedding"
by Harrison Fisher. Back cover: a ca. 1920s wedding card,
both courtesy of Susan Brown Nicholson.

Printed in the United States of America

To order additional copies of this
book or a catalog please contact:

Antique Trader Books
P.O. Box 1050
Dubuque, IA 52004
1-800-334-7165

Antique Trader Books
A division of Landmark Specialty Publications

Dedicated to...

This volume is dedicated to the delights of the mating dance, the joys of romance, the eternal bond between soul mates . . . and to that very first couple, Adam and Eve, who started it all!

CONTENTS

WEDDING TRADITIONS—
HERE COMES THE BRIDE

$\mathcal{A}$CKNOWLEDGMENTS

Robert Ball; Diane Barr, Tracy Lynn Horner, and Julie Dwyer, *Rose D'Zynes*, Vista California; Dorothy Bauer, *A Piece of the Rainbow*, Berkeley, California; Bonnie Luther, Bonnie's Photography Studio, Orange, California; Toby Buonagurio; Dennis Caron; Jill Thomas-Clark, The Corning Museum of Glass, Corning, New York; Gregg Dubbs; Charles Edwards; Kelly Ewing; Alyson French; Charlene Green, The Carlyle, New York; Dorothy Louise Gillette; Cindy Hale, TW, Winchester, Massachusetts; Laura Hall, DeVries Public Relations, New York; Andrew Howard; Betsey Johnson, New York; Joan Castle Joseff; Michele Mathewson; Janet Murphy, Connecticut Historical Society, Hartford, Connecticut; Barbra Music, New York; Donna J. Neary; Susan Brown Nicholson; Polly Pasternak and Sandy Wheeler, Hill-Stead Museum, Farmington, Connecticut; Plaza Hotel, New York; Priscilla of Boston, Charlestown, Massachusetts; Gabrielle Clark, Rituals Photographic Arts, Oceanside, California; Jeannie Roberts, Roberts Antiques, Miscanopy, Florida; Diana Royce, Harriet Beecher Stowe Center, Hartford, Connecticut; Seatyn Ashley Galleries, Lake Arrowhead, California; Frank Shaub, Jr.; Laura Solow, Atlas Floral Decorators, Inc., New York; Jana Starr, Jana Starr Antiques, New York; Catherine Stebeinger, Deep River, Connecticut; Catherine Stein; Dr. and Mrs. Joseph Stolman; Steven Stolman; G. Robert Wagner; Richard A. Watson and Chemical Bank as trustees of the Mark Twain Foundation; Stacey Stolman Webb; Vivienne Westwood, London; Helen Winter Associates, Farmington, Connecticut; Beverly Zell, Mark Twain House, Hartford, Connecticut.

Also to Kyle Husfloen, Editor and Jaro Sebek, Art Director and Designer.

And to the memory of Alan M. Goffman, American Illustration, New York, who was always willing to share his expertise and art treasures with us. He will be missed.

INTRODUCTION

To the Virgins, to Make Much of Time

Gather ye rosebuds while ye may,
Old time is still a-flying
And this same flower that smiles today
Tomorrow will be dying.

Then be not coy, but use your time
And while ye may, go marry;
For having lost but once your prime
You may for ever tarry.

Robert Herrick 1591-1674

"The sum of all that makes a just man happy consists in the well choosing of his wife." . . .

Massinger

Here comes the bride! The powerful sounds of the organ's first triumphal chords resonate throughout the church. The hushed audience turns expectantly awaiting their first glimpse of the blushing bride. This is the ambiance of the wedding day that has been embedded in the customs of much of the civilized world for many decades . . . and throughout centuries long past. Criss-crossing continents, oceans, and cultures, the marriage ceremony is nearly as ancient as time itself.

Etched, hand-colored engraving attributed to an unidentified Viennese artist, circa late 1890s.

Courtesy Dennis Caron

Explaining that "What I do is not about reality. Art and life are very different," Toby Buonagurio—sculptor and professor of art—created this "psychodrama" entitled "The Wedding" in 1990 as part of her ritual series. Standing 16" high with a depth of 10", this work incorporates ceramic with glazes, lusters, acrylic paint, glitter and glass gems. The huge ring at top is fashioned from a crystal doorknob!

Photograph courtesy Toby Buonagurio

RITUALS, SUPERSTITIONS, FRIVOLITY . . . AND ANGST

Perhaps more than other significant occasions (although one cannot overlook the religious and political, such as the coronation of royalty), history reveals that wedding ceremonies and betrothals are steeped in an aura of rituals and superstitions, some sentimental and lovely, others bizarre and amusing. Each era left its distinctive mark on the "marriage bed," for their inhabitants were, even at the higher levels of the social strata, dependent and controlled by the insular and confining world around them. Whether reflective of the peasant or the king, a story emerges, and close examination reveals that each harbored fears and yearnings . . . another mirror to the past.

A romantic nineteenth century painting.

Courtesy Dennis Caron

Each religious, historical, and geographical group had individualized rituals for special occasions, be they sad or happy. Some incorporated symbols of beauty and joy, others were filled with angst and apprehension, and still others straddled a fine line between the two. Many remain a part of modern-day ceremonies, others were slowly abandoned as the worlds of the inhabitants expanded. Whatever the propensity of the participants and their wide-ranging rituals, all provide a further glimpse into their customs and everyday lives.

A stunning example of this is found in Hindu ceremonies, both past and present, which incorporate a beautiful tradition of religious significance as part of the marriage rites. It is the painting ritual that takes place the evening before the ceremony. The bride sits for many hours in an ornate wooden swing while an Indian painter creates elaborate designs on her outstretched palms, using a paste of henna and eucalyptus, which is intermittently daubed with lemon juice and sugar to heighten the sepia-brown color. Resembling ornate lace work, these paintings contain signficant Hindu symbols and hidden names, all of which slowly fade over the next few weeks. To further enhance the beauty of a Hindu ceremony, the bride arrives at the wedding site in a *dholi*—a canopied carriage borne on the shoulders of the male members of the wedding party. The groom's entrance is equally dramatic, for he rides to the nuptials on a white steed that is covered with flowers.

The rituals of the Elizabethan wedding are representative of the playful side of the marital coin, for the mainstay of these earthy folks was "the pleasure principle," with the ensuing frivolity mirroring the earthy existence of the peasants, who then made up the majority of the population. Pretentiousness, accompanied by inordinate amounts of food

The Behaim Beaker, circa 1495, Venice, Italy. Colorless glass, blown, enameled and gilded, this is thought to be the beaker made for the July 7, 1495 wedding of Michael Behaim of the Behaim family of Nuremburg and Catherine Lochner, the daughter of a rich merchant. This view depicts the Archangel Michael slaying the dragon; the other sides show arms of the Behaim family and St. Catherine.
Photograph courtesy The Corning Museum of Glass

"Courting in the French court"—Bisque figurines in period costume.

and drink, were the order of the day (and in some cases, days!). Although the elite could always avail themselves of more exclusive amenities, here, for the most part, were common folk who lived under circumstances demanding their own ingenuity when it came to celebrating important occasions. In essence, they created their own "fun."

As might be expected, romance—with all its heady expectations—was at the center of these rituals. The bridesmaids carefully tied "love knots" (pieces of colorful ribbon representing the wedding tie) all over the bride's gown. Each color had a symbolic meaning, although hues were frequently contradictory, signifying a positive force to one group, but a negative one to another. Hence, ribbons of certain colors might appear on one gown but be totally shunned on another. In this traditional display of "foppish" finery, the groom was not relegated to a "back seat," for he too was gussied up with ribbons that would complement his bride. Woe to the bridesmaids whose fingers weren't agile, for in addition to knotting ribbons for the wedding party, they also fashioned garlands of flowers to decorate the house.

The Old Goblet, circa 1773-1774, Manheim, Pennsylvania, American Flint Glass Manufactory of Henry William Stiegel; engraved by Lazarus Isaacs. Colorless and opaque white glass, blown and engraved to mark the marriage of Stiegel's daughter Elizabeth and William Old.
Photograph courtesy The Corning Museum of Glass

A wonderfully romantic illustration by Brunelleschi, circa 1915-1925.

Romance on canvas . . . Des Pastorales, a print from the series by Watteau, Boucher, and Fragonard.

The bride of Medieval France.

☙ *"By the time of Plato in the fifth century B.C., the taking of a wife had become for many a regrettable, if necessary, burden."*[1]

☙ *In Roman times, the simple tunic worn by the bride was belted with a "knot of Hercules," which could only be untied by the eager bridegroom.*

☙ *The pre-Christian Middle Eastern Essenes permitted couples to live together without marriage so long as there was no pregnancy, in which case the marriage was then solemnized.*

☙ *"In Yorkshire, England, a man could announce a trial marriage by saying, 'If my bride becomes pregnant, I shall take her'."*[2]

☙ *German peasants were permitted to spend several "trial" nights with a marriage prospect, moving to another if the results weren't satisfactory. This custom was understandably abused as the males flitted from one "possibility" to another, but nonetheless the practice continued well into the nineteenth century.*

☙ *"The Puritans put a cloud over love and the rakes of the Restoration put a cloud over marriage."*[3]

Serenading his lady love—Oil on Board painting entitled "He Sang for Her As . . . " by Howard Pyle (1853-1911). Originally featured as part of "The Story of Adhelmar," *Harper's Monthly,* April 1904.
Photograph courtesy Alan M. Goffman,
American Illustration

In Scotland during the Middle Ages, couples made a pledge whereby they were given permission to live together for a year and a day, after which they could decide whether or not they wished to formally marry.

Although tying shoes to the bumpers of newlyweds' vehicles was common in the twentieth century, shoes had been incorporated into the festivities of Ancient Greece many centuries before, but in a more robust manner; the embellishments on an early vase depict the departure of the bride and groom—and a shoe flying at their heads!

The vow of a bride of the Middle Ages included the promise to be "bonny and buxom in bed and at board,"[4] one that fell from disfavor and was replaced with the less hearty "meek and obedient."

Divorce was made easy after the Russian Revolution, for either party could announce their intention by simply sending the other a postcard! "This practice was outlawed when it became apparent that far too many divorced Russians were unaware of their status, which, of course may have been more the fault of the Russian postal system than of a loose divorce law."[5]

Flipping that marital coin to the other side, the European Jewish wedding of the Middles Ages bore more resemblance to a funeral than a joyous occasion. Here the bride covered her wedding finery with a white shroud of mourning, signifying the ". . . destruction of Zion, the dispersal of the Israelites, and the subsequent history of racial grief."[6] Not to be outdone, the groom also covered himself with a similar "hood of mourning." The glasses from which this somber wedding couple sipped were smashed against the wall of the synagogue—a custom that was later refined to the present tradition of trampling them underfoot. The power of the lowly foot was carried one step further, for both Medieval Jews and most Christians believed that if the groom's right foot was firmly planted atop his bride's left foot during the ceremony he was assured future dominance over her!

Design drawing for the traditional Jewish ceremony, complete with flower-bedecked *chupah*, majestic columns topped with greenery and tall candles, and the laurel chains and candles that decorated the aisle.

Design drawing courtesy of Laura Solow, Atlas Floral Decorations, Inc.

Selected clauses in marriage contracts as attributed to Time *magazine in the 1978 edition of* People's Almanac #2:

1. *Husband will lift the toilet seat before urinating.*
2. *Wife will not say she does not believe her husband loves her.*
3. *Ralph agrees not to pick, nag, or comment about Wanda's skin blemishes.*
4. *Wanda will refrain from yelling about undone chores until Sunday afternoon.*[7]

THE RING:
WEDDING AND BETROTHAL

"To the dusky sirens of the Nile, legend tells us, we owe the custom of symbolizing the marriage vows with a ring. In hieroglyphics, the Egyptians carved a circle to represent eternity as being round, hence endless. It is not surprising, therefore, that the circular form was regarded by them as emblematic of marriage ties, signifying that mutual love and affection should flow from man to wife as in a circle, continually and forever."

"Wedding Ring Sentiment" booklet, circa 1927

The ring has been a token of commitment between husbands and wives, and brides and grooms "to be" for many centuries. However, the types of rings in favor—just like fashion—changed drastically over time. In fact, wedding and "commitment" rings were not always made of particularly valuable materials, as is generally the case today. For many, it was the thought that counted—and there were, indeed, many of those. Each style reflected the predilections of the inhabitants of a given era. Each was also usually presented as a token of love and a treasured romantic gesture—but, as you will see, not always!

WEDDING RINGS

The marriage contract during fifth century B.C. Greece was only verbal and not in writing. Nevertheless, a public verbal declaration was considered a binding oath, predicated on the honor of the participants. This was also true in the Middle Ages, when only the ring served as proof of the ceremony and, until the latter period of the Middle Ages, the mere uttering of "I do marry you" became the sole binding agent to make a marriage legal. In many of these cultures, a man's word was his bond. In fact, the word "wedding" comes from the Anglo-Saxon word "wedd," which means "to make a solemn pledge."

These same ancient Greek cultures believed that the heart and ring finger were blessed with a special connection via the vein that ran between the two, the heart signifying love and the finger signifying the commitment of the ring. "Mabrobius, in his *Saturnalia* alludes to the belief in the following words: '. . . because of this nerve, the newly betrothed places the ring on this finger of his spouse, as though it were a representation of the heart.' Macrobius asserts that he derived his information from an Egyptian priest."[8]

Etruscan
Wedding ring mounted with a dove. A wealth of wonderful designs has been left to us by ancient Etruria

The illustrations in this section taken from the 1927 booklet, "Wedding Ring Sentiment."

Nonetheless, there are conflicting assertions as to why the wedding ring was worn on the third finger of the left hand. In Christian ceremonies, the priest touched one finger when he intoned, "In the name of the father," the next finger with "of the son," and the third finger, upon which the ring was placed, when he completed "and of the Holy Ghost." The ring didn't necessarily remain there, however, for during the time of George I of England, the thumb became the favorite resting place—perhaps the bigger the ring the better and, thus, one that would fit only on the largest digit. There is also evidence that during the fifteenth century the ring rested on the bride's right hand, not the left, and even in earlier times and following, the favored finger covered the entire gamut of digits—from thumb, to middle finger, to right hand, to left. Not to be outdone, early twentieth century Arabs in Tunis continued the custom of placing the wedding ring on the first finger of the left hand.

An early Byzantine wedding ring dating from about 400 A.D. is most unusual, featuring a bicephalic (two heads). It was circular with male and female busts facing each other and the religious symbol of the cross over their heads. Another ancient wedding ring of Roman origin, probably from the fifth century A.D., had a square bezel, also with two romantic figures—this time a warrior resting on his lance and his lady-love with arms outstretched to him.

Ancient Hebrew
A temple dome adorned the wedding ring and covered a gold plate inscribed "Mazel Tob"

Wedding rings were not always of valuable materials. In early Roman times, women wore gold wedding rings only in public. In the confines of their homes, the more elaborate and showy gold ring was replaced by a plain circlet of unset iron. "During the 19th and even into the 20th century, rings of iron remained in favor especially in Germany, where many were used as wedding rings. The inevitable problem of rust stains was finally solved during the early years of the 20th century when a thin layer of gold was added to the inside."[9] Between this seemingly minute amount of gold and that found in the rings of solid gold that always remained popular, it is estimated that during the First World War over a million dollars was realized from the melted gold of the rings donated by patriotic Germans for the war effort.

A ring of any kind presented a financial burden in some areas of Ireland and England during the early part of the twentieth century, and the rental of gold wedding rings by those too poor to purchase them became a booming business. On an assembly-line basis, devoid of any sentimentality, the ring was returned after the ceremony only to find its way to another finger on another day. Softening the blow somewhat was the belief in certain quarters that to wear a borrowed ring was actually a symbol of good luck.

Grecian
Wedding ring has Greek inscription. Exact date, unknown

In other more affluent societies, gold and platinum (called the "metal of heaven") were, and continue to be, desirable choices for the traditional wedding ring, with platinum reaching its peak of popularity during the early and Deco years of the twentieth century.

BETROTHAL RINGS

In many cultures, betrothal rings—an early version of today's engagement ring—bore as much if not more importance than the wedding ring, and they remained in favor until about the time of the Reformation in England. As early as the fifth century A.D., the law of the Visigoths was clear as to the significance of the betrothal ring. It read, " 'Since there are many who, forgetful of their plighted faith, defer the fulfillment of their nuptial contracts, this license should be suppressed'."[10] This ensured that once this public declaration had been witnessed and the ring given to the prospective bride, it was unquestioned that the marriage ceremony would follow unless both parties agreed to "call the whole thing off." Here was a situation where a reluctant bridegroom or bride understood all too late the adage, "Act in haste, repent at leisure," or, better yet, never!

From very early times it was common practice to have religious and other sentiments (or lack of them) inscribed on the inside of marital or betrothal rings. An inscription in a Greek betrothal ring of the fourth century B.C. reads, "To her who excells not only in virtue and prudence, but also in wisdom." Another espouses, "I rejoice in the gift because of the affection of the giver." One unearthed from ancient Rome was more than a bit ambivalent, for it read simply, "Love me, I will love thee." At the other end of the spectrum, a thirteenth century Gothic ring was simply but lovingly inscribed, "In me is fidelity," while an old French inscription reads, "My heart is rejoiced, and so it should be, if God aid me, For I feel I could not have chosen better."

Others were more concerned with personal retribution, like the one from 1646 that read, "I love the rod and thee and God," or the ominous, "Be truly wise lest death surprise." On the other hand, the inscriptions that read "A loving wife prolongeth life," and "Death never parts such loving hearts" were a bit more uplifting. And then there was the philosophical, "Ryches be unstable, and beauty will dekay, but faithful love will ever last, till death dryve it away."

Versions of this same style continued into the sixteenth and seventeenth centuries (which seemed particularly obsessed with them) and were called "poesy" rings. However, the ambiguities of their verses finally doomed them to temporary

Roman

This Roman wedding ring found in Swarthe, France, inscribed with names of bride and groom. Fifth century

German

Wedding ring with precious stones inscribed, "What God hath joined together, let no man put asunder." Sixteenth century

disfavor. Many of the aforementioned romantic gestures took a strange twist, resulting in not only heady sentiments but emotional highs and lows, to wit:

> *"Our contract was heaven's act"*
> *"In thee my choice do I rejoice"*
> *"I will be yours while life endures"*
> *And the rather ominous, "If you deny, then sure I die"*
> *"I did commit no act of folly, when I married my sweet Molly"*
> *"'Tis fit no man should be alone, which made Tom to marry Joan"*
> *And the oddly convoluted, "We strangely met, and so do many, but now as true as ever any."*

These were joined by some from the "tell it like it is" school of thought:

> *"Faithful but unhappy"*
> *"Ultimate good, not present pleasure"*
> *"If I think my wife is fair, what need other people care."*

And the supreme "putdown":

> *"Thou wert not handsome, wise, but rich; 'twas that which did my eye bewitch."*

The Middle Ages favored gimmel rings, a design that consisted of not one, but two or even three intertwining circlets, which served as symbols of the complex interaction between eternity and the marital joys of the heart. Carrying that concept even further, in the seventeenth century, one style of betrothal ring was called a "puzzle ring" because of its six intertwining hoops, all under the watchful eye of an angel's head. Three of the hoops featured enameling, two had clasped hands (signifying betrothal), and the remaining was a key, long symbolic of the opening of a household.

The use of gemstones in betrothal rings also assumed significance into the twentieth century. "Regard" rings were quite popular early on and were set with the following stones, the first letter of which formed the word "regard": ruby, emerald, garnet, amethyst, ruby, and diamond. If one was fortunate enough to have a workable first name—like Sophia, for

> ⚜ *Slapping, pushing, and hitting at a wedding?! In the Middle Ages, yes. All were part of the audience's expected response when the ring was placed on the bride's finger.*

Saxon
Wedding ring from an old sepulchre at Harnham Hill, England. Seventh century

Fifteenth Century English
Heart on the opposite side, inscribed "God Helps"

instance—the ring could contain a sapphire, opal, peridot, hyalite, iolite, and amethyst.

Inscriptions that consisted of the random interlocking of the wedding couple's names into a conglomeration of seemingly meaningless letters also enjoyed popularity, even into this century. For instance, Miriam and Robert would appear as *rMoAbIeRrItM*, with one name reading from left to right and the other from right to left!

In nineteenth century America, the symbolism of the ring also applied to courtship rules. In fact, these guidelines were quite explicit:

> *"If a gentleman wants a wife, he wears a ring on the first finger of the left hand. If he is engaged, he wears it on the second finger. If married, he wears it on the third finger. When a lady is not engaged, she wears a hoop or diamond on her first finger. If engaged, she wears it upon the second finger. If she intends to remain a maid, she wears her ring upon her fourth finger. Thus, by a few simple tokens, the passion of love is expressed."*[11]

And lastly, love, romance, and social amenities aside, one particular scenario involving the ring reached heights of inventiveness and ingenuity that future centuries (luckily!) were never able to equal. For during the Manx period on the Isle of Man, ". . . if a man was found guilty of having done injury to a maiden, the latter was given a sword, a rope and a ring, signifying that she could either have him beheaded, or hung, or else could force him to wed her. That the last-mentioned choice was the one most frequently made is most probable, as the rehabilitation of her good name thus attained might well outweigh any satisfaction to be gained from the exercise of revenge."[12]

English
This wedding ring was inscribed with a love "poesy." Seventeenth century

Old French
Inscribed—It is spoken—she holds me. Fifteenth century

Advice regarding betrothal rings came from all quarters, extending even into royalty. A letter written in Ghent in 1477 by Dr. Wilhelm Moroltinger to Archduke Maximilian (who would later become Emperor) prior to his vow of betrothal to Mary of Burgundy advised him to extend his generosity beyond a mere gold ring by also presenting her with one inset with a diamond, and then showering her with costly jeweled baubles.

A JOURNEY THROUGH PERIODICALS OF THE DAY:

❦ *The April 1923 issue of* Vogue *stated that "A wedding ring that is sufficiently conservative and yet unusual is a circlet of diamonds with diamond drops."*

❦ *"Just now pearls are favored for engagement rings—a single perfect pearl mounted in a slender hoop of platinum, sometimes with an oblong diamond on each side."*

Harper's Bazar, *May 1923*

❦ *In the April 1939 issue of* Vogue *one could find very, very wide wedding bands . . . plain ones in red gold almost to the knuckle were $45; narrower styles were in green gold at $35, and twice those amounts if in platinum.*

❦ *Touted in the June 1940 issue of* Mademoiselle *were nine-stone wedding bands with fish tail designs in 14 karat natural gold at $40, or a seven-stone beauty, channel set in 24 karat gold, for $24.*

THE VEIL

Contradictory to what is generally considered its purpose in modern times, the bridal veil wasn't always intended to romantically obscure the bride's face from the groom until they were man and wife. In places like Morocco and Ancient India, it was considered a necessary protection from the bride's supposed "evil eye," a condition that only the purification of the marriage ceremony could alleviate. The evil eye was no laughing matter, for it was feared that to gaze on her prior to the ceremony could place not only the groom but others in the audience in harm's way. Even in ancient Rome, brides preferred deep red veils, since these face coverings were also purported to prevent malevolent influences from harming the unwary groom . . . and even the assembled guests. Fear of evil influences didn't end there, for preceding the bridal couple in the procession that escorted them to their new home was a flame bearer holding aloft a torch of white thorns. Serving to ward off evil and ensure tranquility, it was used to light the hearth when they entered.

Such afflictions aside, other cultures took a more gentle view of the veil's significance, considering it a protective influence on the bride's innocence. The veil assumed such importance, in fact, that early Christians made it obligatory for potential brides to wear them from the time of betrothal until the actual ceremony.

This 1936 print features a magnificent floral veil, accented by similar blossoms at the gown's neckline.

In an attempt to "do things their own way," many eighteenth century English brides surprisingly chose to discard veils altogether. Several generations later, Victorian women found their grandmothers' relaxed attitudes somewhat "loose"—especially when it related to something as important as the wedding ceremony—and once again restored the veil to its ritualistic position of purity in the wedding ritual.

From the 1950s, a ceramic bust replete with ornate bridal headdress.

Veil of the 1920s . . . with a Russian influence, this veil has a transparent cap of loosely-wrapped tulle decorated with a cluster of orange blossoms and lilies.

A sketch based on a scene titled "La Coiffeuse" (The Hairdresser), shows tall French seventeenth century brides' bonnets topped by high hairdos called *fantanges marches*, trimmed with corsages and drapes of fine lace. From the period of Louis XIV.

Right: French, circa 1910, this bridal headpiece of wax flowers and leaves adapts well to the naturalistic, Art Nouveau influence of the period.
Bottom Left: Circa late 1950s, a pearl and rhinestone hat by Mr. John made a most charming wedding headdress.
Bottom right: Not just for royalty anymore! Here a rhinestone tiara headdress, circa 1950 . . . all the rage after the coronation of Queen Elizabeth II and the wedding of Princess Grace (nee Kelly) in Monaco.

Courtesy Jana Starr Antiques

A JOURNEY THROUGH
PERIODICALS OF THE DAY

The May 1923 issue of Harper's Bazar *featured a beautiful model wearing a Molyneaux wedding veil . . . a misty bit of tulle held close to the head with double strands of pearls across the forehead and at the crown, matching the long, long ropes of triple strand pearls encircling the bride's neck and falling to her waist. Other veils in the same issue displayed: A similar tulle design held by an orange-blossom bandeau; a sophisticated turban of silver tissue and orange blossoms by Lucille; and a medieval design of pearls and white beads fitted over the forehead, with a jeweled band encircling the head to hold the veil in place. A similar design had a diaphanous diadem of lace to secure the veil; however, it also featured a novel and exotically attractive "two-for-one" addition, for along with the traditional long veil another short one covered the area from the bride's forehead to the tip of her nose, reminding one of the mysterious beauty in a Persian harem.*

According to a 1930s issue of Vogue, *"Nine out of ten city brides wear lace veils, and no brides of to-day follow the old mode of wearing a veil over the face. The sentiment which this stands for is so picturesque that it seems a pity to abandon it."*

Top right: From a 1920s print, this bride appears in profile to better display her charmingly-wrapped veil with floral banding. The huge pearls (at least 12mm) are undoubtedly genuine.

Middle right: A breathless bridal beauty, her cloche headdress is typical of the 1920s.

Above: The veil worn here by a bride of 1912 is reputed to have cost $2,000—an enormous sum under any circumstances, and even more extravagant considering what a single dollar could purchase in 1913! *The Designer,* April 1913.

Left: Chic bridal headdress from the April 1931 issue of La Coiffure Parisienne Illustree. Creations de Ch. Sezille.

THE ROMANCE OF ORANGE BLOSSOMS

"It is interesting to recall that both Milton and Spencer held the opinion that the orange was the 'golden apple' presented by Juno to Jupiter on the day of their nuptials . . ."

"Wedding Ring Sentiment" booklet, circa 1927

Throughout much of history, the orange blossom has been associated with a message of romance and marriage. In Crete, the bride and bridegroom were sprinkled with orange flower water; in Sardinia, oranges were hung upon the horns of the oxen that pulled the nuptial carriage.

"The hopes of a prosperous marriage were expressed by the use of these flowers. Although the orange tree was brought to England as early as 1290, it was not until the 16th century that there was ever any real cultivation of it there . . . Many, indeed, hold that it was introduced by Sir Walter Raleigh and then not from any Saracen land, but from India or the Far East. A second theory is that orange blossoms came to be worn by the brides at their marriage because the flowers were not only scented but were also rare and costly and, therefore, within the reach of only the rich and noble, thus signifying the bride to be of high rank."

"Wedding Ring Sentiment" booklet, circa 1927

The bridal wreath in many incarnations: old wax flowers and leaves in the shape of orange blossoms (from France, circa 1910-1920), silk flowers, dried flowers, porcelain flowers, and pearls.
Courtesy Jana Starr Antiques

Which country or area incorporated this fragrant flower into the wedding ceremony remains contested, for it is also posited that, since it was a citrus product indigenous to the area, the use of ceremonial orange blossoms originated in Spain.

Wedding cake masterpieces of today: Several examples of the beauty and originality possible with wedding cake presentations. Those shown here are either fondant-covered or butter cream with various flavored tiers, like lemon, raspberry, whipped cream, chocolate mousse or chocolate fudge. Several have a combination of real and confectionary flowers, such as the one with large sugar cabbage roses on top to complement the real ones around the base; another has a sugar monogram at its peak designed to match the invitations and Tiffany menu cards; the sailboat motif atop yet another romantically signifies the sailboat on which the future bride and groom became engaged!

Photographs courtesy Catherine Stebinger Cake Designs

*T*HE ICING ON THE CAKE
(And Rice on the Head)

The tradition of a wedding cake is *de rigeur* as part of the modern-day reception. However, its roots are steeped in history. There is even a connection between the rice ceremoniously tossed at the bride and groom following the ceremony and . . . cake! Today we throw rice as the newlyweds depart. In Elizabethan times, this ceremonial rite of passage was delayed until the bride entered her home, generally the site of the after-ceremony frivolity. Then, however, instead of rice, tiny cakes were tossed at the wedding couple, again assuming varying interpretations of symbolic significance. Some revelers ". . . passed the pieces of cake through their wedding rings. Still others, believing that the presence of these broken cakes would help ease the defloration of the bride, scattered cake crumbs on the new couple during the wedding feast."[13] Unlike the wedding receptions of today, these celebrations generally continued for days . . . and even weeks!

In ancient Rome, the bride and groom shared a wheat cake and, as we do even now, after the wedding feast everyone partook of a piece of the more traditional wedding cake. The cake is the outgrowth of its commonest denominator, grain . . . and from there to grain's relationship to fertility. Indeed, the notion that grain and cakes played a symbolic role in the wedding rites goes back to antiquity, where marriage customs in many countries and civilizations were understandably related to fertility, symbolizing their hopes for an abundance of crops . . . and babies! An example of this use of inanimate objects in the marriage ritual can be found in Java, where, prior to the harvest, wedding couples fashioned of simple ears of rice were joined together just like real-life brides and grooms. These "rice newlyweds" were then ensconced in a special corner of a barn, surrounded by equally inanimate guests—large sheaves of rice! To prevent anything from disturbing this important ritual, the barn itself was verboten to humans for forty days. In much the same way, natives of Northwestern India used wooden wedding dolls, representing the rain gods, in an attempt to ensure the fertility of their harvest.

In Hindu ceremonies, the bride was given to her groom by the mother, following which the wedding couple ritualistically walked around the sacred fire seven times. To express his hopes for fertility, the groom's brother then participated by tossing grain each time they passed him.

During the Middle Ages, there were similar superstitions relating to grain and the harvest, for when the bride and groom entered their home they were pelted with seeds as the jolly participants called out, "Plenty . . . plenty." However, their entreaties met with little success, for as one thirteenth century observer wrote, "In some parts I have seen how when women came home from church after a wedding, others threw corn in their faces as they entered their house, crying plenty! plenty! Yet for all this . . . they remained poor . . . and had no abundance of goods whatsoever."[14]

Now preserved in a glass dome, these edible confections decorated the top of a 1970s wedding cake.

A memento for the guests . . . from 1921, this ribboned box still contains a piece of wedding cake.

Victorians brought the wedding cake into the twentieth century as an art form . . . and also as an ingenious memento of the occasion, for the cake was often surrounded by tiny boxes, decorated and tied with ribbon, which held an additional sampling for each guest to take when they departed. Often, in a display of Victorian opulence, they spared no expense for either! "One famous wedding cake with the pile of small boxes ran up to $2,500. The caterer had used not only fruits but rare liquor in making the cake, and employed a sculptor to design the towering decoration."

"Hail to the Easter Bride" *by Kate Hopkins.*
The Designer, *April 1913*

A playful cupid, surrounded by a trellis of lilies of the valley, sits atop this composition wedding cake topper.

Courtesy Jana Starr Antiques

This sophisticated wedding-cake couple stand beneath a hand-crocheted trellis.

Theodate Pope wrote the following entry in her diary the night before her cousin's 1900 wedding . . . "This evening we had such fun putting the wedding cakes in the boxes. We all sat around the dining room table and worked as systematically as shop girls."[15]

Rare for the 1920s period, a beautifully hand painted, celluloid black couple. (Note the groom's spats!)

Very chic . . . he with a farmer's Levi-inspired "tux," she with mummy-like wrapping, veiling, and flowers. Of composition and bisque, both have real hair!

Classic "kewpie" bisque figurals from the 1920s-30s period.

⚜ *The Victorians are also credited with a custom that added a decorative touch to the wedding cake and at the same time cleverly gifted each of the bride's attendants. Ribbons (one for each attendant) were placed between the cake's layers, and each bridesmaid randomly chose one to remove. Silver charms of different designs (to later hang from a neck chain) were attached to the end that remained hidden, thus serving as a fond and lasting remembrance of the happy occasion. Called "cake pulls," the idea is attracting renewed interest in the 1990s, adding something "new" to the reception festivities and "spicing up" the wedding cake at the same time!*

German-made bride and groom celluloid "kewpie" cake toppers, circa 1930s.

DOWRIES, MATCHMAKING . . . AND WORSE

"The Bachelor's Song"

How happy a thing were a wedding
And a bedding;
If a man might purchase a wife
For a twelvemonth and a day;
but to live with her all a man's life,
For ever and for ay,
Till she grow as grey as a cat
Good faith, Mr. Parson, I thank you for that.

Thomas Flatman (1637-1688)

Encompassing many cultures on many continents, the ritual of the dowry spanned countless centuries, offering further insight into the structures that were predominant within not only the country but also its religious and social groups.

A bride admiring her trousseau.
From an 1880s German magazine.

In ancient Greece the dowry served a dual purpose . . . with a "boomerang" quality . . . for if the wife divorced her husband and returned to her father's house, the dowry had to be returned from whence it came. This undoubtedly suppressed the divorce rate, while contributing to an inordinate number of marriages by pretense. "Plutarch tells how Alcibiades, most prodigal of the Athenians, boldly kidnapped his neglected wife from the very courtroom where she was seeking a divorce . . . It wasn't that he loved her and could not live without her; he had already spent the dowry."[1]

Early Jewish lore indicates that the purchase of a wife—a sum no less than two shekels—validated the marriage. Being without funds did not, however, inhibit a man's ability to marry, for he could actually "work off" a fair amount in the father's employ. The bride's father was, in fact, a major player in this tableau, for the choice of husband rested totally with him, the bride having little, and usually no, influence as to the final outcome.

Matchmaking was also an important part of the pre-marriage bargaining. European Jews of the Middle Ages employed professional matchmakers, called *shadchans*. Since travel between communities was, at best, difficult, and seriously inhibited the possibility of meeting potential marriage candidates, the matchmaker became an irreplaceable commodity. The *shadchan* was most often just a mobile tradesperson, earning additional sums by using his accessibility to homes in outlying areas as a "foot in the door" for finding "just the right bride, for just the right groom, at just the right price!"

In this atmosphere of dowries and matchmaking, even the ring came with "strings attached." An old German betrothal formula bluntly stated, "I give you this ring as a sign of the marriage which has been promised between us," and then proceeded to destroy whatever romantic notion was intended by continuing, ". . . provided your father gives you a marriage portion of 1000 reichsthalers."2

The value of the dowry turned ugly during the Middle Ages when the lords searched among their subjects for all available widows and orphaned daughters, for they could then marry them off and thereby claim a share of the dowry that would have, under normal circumstances, gone to the now deceased fathers. Unpleasant though it is, history is burdened with such tales, encompassing diverse cultures throughout the world.

An even crueler practice than negotiating within families and groups with money and goods, kidnapping outright or both kidnapping and selling on the auction block was yet another odious example of women being viewed as economic property—to be bartered and, in effect, sold to the highest bidder. Over two thousand years ago, Herodotus wrote of the gathering of marriageable Babylonian girls onto a town "auction block." Always the salesman, the auctioneer displayed the most comely of the group first, eliminating them one by one until he'd reached the female who, woefully, gave his eyes the least pleasure.

"Courting." A scene of Chinese lovers by Henry J. Soulen. Oil on board.
Courtesy of Alan M. Goffman, American Illustration

Unlike many cultures that sanctioned brides of only eleven or twelve, the early Middle Ages saw the church valiantly, but often unsuccessfully, decreeing that all brides must have reached the age of fifteen. Even the purity of the cradled infant wasn't excluded from this bartering, for in some cultures babies were actually betrothed to each other and from that time forward spent their childhoods as companions in the same household. Surprisingly, this practice continued in some areas of rural England into the nineteenth century, with these betrothed children even sharing the same bed. On the other hand, Hindu cultures generally insisted that the young girl-child return to her father's house until she was of child-bearing age. Like many patriarchs in cultures before him, a Hindu father of several centuries ago also considered finding a mate for his daughter both a personal and social challenge. It was imperative that his choice be made before she was ten but, "Ten was cutting it rather fine; the rewards were higher but so were the risks. Wrote a Hindu sage: 'He who gives a girl of eight in marriage attains heaven; the giver of a girl of nine attains a higher heaven; the giver of a girl who has attained the tenth year, but not puberty, is given a place in the highest heaven; and the giver of a mature woman is condemned to hell.' His advise was not ignored."3

Fathers weren't the only family members to exert their influence. In Uganda, the prospective suitor was expected to approach the older brother and paternal uncle of his chosen one. When the meeting took place it was replete with nuance and ritual, for the prospective bride was then asked to pour beer, her actions thereby indicating her feelings . . . if she agrees to serve, she's indicating her consent, and the three parties are then free to negotiate outside her presence. This bartering included offers of livestock, food, and cloth, all of which became a significant factor as to how the male, and the community, viewed the young woman. "Among the Kiffirs, six cattle is regarded as about the minimum price for a homely girl with a bad temper, and thirty cattle are enough for an energetic beauty."[4]

The need to maintain one's dignity played a role in dowry negotiations, and ingenuity in the face of adversity was no stranger to the matchmaking process. This may have reached its apex in one region of India where ". . . parents of daughters who have no chance at a wealthy bridegroom save face by first 'marrying' a girl to a bunch of flowers, which are then thrown down a well. Now she is a 'widow,' and her parents can accept a nominal brideprice for her without shame."[5]

In all cultures it was understandable that the health of the female under consideration was also an important negotiating tool, for life was tenuous and devastating medical scourges were destined to attack the young brides of centuries past. Many died during pregnancy and childbirth, others fell prey to plagues and tuberculosis. Most did not live long and, so, to have at least the possibility of a wife who would enjoy good health was a highly-prized attribute.

An amusing tale involving "checking out the potential bride" clearly indicated the importance of the dowry, even among royalty. In 1505, when Henry VII was contemplating marriage to the widowed Queen of Naples, whom he had never seen, he sent his emissaries to make a lengthy inspection, to wit: ". . . to mark and note well the age and stature . . . and the features of her body . . . whether she be painted or not . . . whether . . . fat or lean, sharp or round . . . cheerful and amiable, frowning or melancholy . . . see her hands bare and to note . . . to whether her hands be fat or lean, long or short . . . ."[6] Determined to leave no stone unturned, the King's instructions continued, advising the emissaries to check whether there were any hairs around her lips and the "condition" of her breath. Not satisfied that even these reports be truthful, Henry, as a final resort, insisted that they commission a portrait of the Queen, so he could view her for himself. Bent upon maintaining her aura of mystery, she initially foiled their attempts by swaddling herself in layers of fabric. Eventually, the emissaries were able to give the King a positive report. It was all to no avail for, in the meantime, Henry had discovered that his prospective bride was essentially without funds, and thus, "when push came to shove" outward amenities were outweighed by financial considerations, and the poor (but probably "lucky") Queen of Naples remained husbandless!

Taking a dispassionate look at reality wasn't lost on the sensibilities of poets of the day, who penned "no holds barred" verse comparing how the female chose to be seen by her suitor or husband and how his jaundiced eye might have more realistically viewed her; to wit, this example titled "Phillis's Age," by Matthew Prior (1664-1721):

> How old may Phillis be, you ask,
> whose beauty thus all hearts engage?
> To answer is no easy task:
> For she has really two ages.

"I am not one of those who do not believe in love at first sight, but I believe in taking a second look."

H. Vincent

Unattached women in Zulu tribes communicated their availability and feelings via the colors of their tribal beads: white signified love, purity and hope; black, marriage; red, anger; green, jealously or depression; pink, poverty and despondency (no attempt to "gild the lily" here!); and yellow a signal that they had wealth and cattle!

Stiff in brocade, and inch'd in stays,
Her patches, paint, and jewels on;
all day let envy view her face,
and Phillis is but twenty-one.

Paint, patches, jewels laid aside,
At night astronomers agree,
the evening has the day belied;
And Phillis is some forty-three.

Even Chaucer made caustic observations on the wedded state when he wrote in *The Cantebury Tales,* "She was a worthy woman all her live, Husband at the church door had she five." John Dryden, on the other hand, traveled from church door to graveyard when he penned the following epitaph for his wife: "Here lies my wife; here let her lie! Now she's a peace and so am I."

But one would be hard pressed to equal this unintendedly lusty observation regarding the strange custom that many American Puritan immigrants brought with them from the Old World—one made doubly so by their own rigid sexual mores. Called "bundling," it was a strictly localized ritual whereby young people got to "know" each other in the warmth of a single bed, although most frequently with a restrictive board between them. One Puritan poet, fire and brimstone emanating from his pen, expounded:

"Down deep in hell there let them dwell
And bundle on that Bed.
There burn and roll without control
Till all their lusts are fed."[7]

Courting and marriage were not happy times for these folks, for, facing harsh realities head on—and not to be outdone by their forebears across the ocean—the American Pilgrims found marriage to be a necessity for survival in the New World, and the unmarried of either sex were treated with contempt. "In America, women comprised only ten percent of the population by 1642. Supply would not match demand for more than two centuries."[8] These folks were in such a hurry to enter the state of matrimony that the wedding generally occurred a mere eight days after the announcement of intent. Since this austere society forbade fashionable finery and jewelry, the ceremonies were somber affairs, lacking the beauty and pomp of most of their European counterparts.

During this same period in Canada, the situation was handled dispassionately and with haste, with the French regularly dispatching vessels filled with maidens to serve as potential marriage partners for their lonely countrymen across the sea (proving to be an onimously apt forerunner to the unflattering "meat market" term of later years). "The contemporary historian LaHoutan wrote a vivid description of the arrival of a bridal vessel: 'Severy Ships were sent higher from France with a Cargoe of Women of an ordinary Reputation, under the Direction of some old stale Nuns, who rang'd them in three Classes. The Vestal Virgins were heap'd up (if I may so speak) one above another, in three different Apartments where the Bridegrooms singled out their Brides, just as a Butcher does a Ewe amongst a flock of Sheep.' "[9] All was frequently not well for the males involved either. Penalties for lagging behind in choosing a wife were destined to affect those areas where they would do the most harm—and be most apt to get the laggard's attention. Retribution was swift, and the poor fellow was given only fifteen days to "bite the bullet" after the first choices were presented to him. Not to do so incurred the wrath of one's peers

The German-Swiss Amish and Mennonite sects (commonly referred to as the Pennsylvania Dutch) have made determination of the marital status of their males both simple and foolproof. Eligible males are clean shaven, married ones have full beards! (No chance here to fool fair damsel!)

As late as the early twentieth century, a love-based marriage in Korea was considered no marriage at all, and those who "crossed the line" were considered to have entered into an illegitimate union and seriously punished.

"According to an ancient English law, a new husband was responsible for his bride's previous debts unless he married her in her shift or chemise on the King's highway. There are several cases on record of this mysterious rule being carried out to the letter."[10]

and, more importantly, the loss of livelihood—a far more severe punishment—for he was then forbidden to enter the woods, engage in Indian trade, or even hunt and fish. Considering the alternative—no matter his choice—matrimony must surely have looked better and better!

Women—and consequently potential wives—were just as scarce a commodity in the nineteenth century American West, with the ambiance there differing greatly from that to be found in the more genteel Eastern society. Newspapers regularly advertised for women. "In 1867, for instance, the *Iowa Reporter* summoned women to that state, claiming that the territory was 'sixty thousand short of women to make the balance equal.' "[11]

Loss of legal freedom was a factor of married life, even in this century. As described in the May 1923 issue of *Harper's Bazar,* "In France the *mariage de convenance* still exists. French parents with a marriageable daughter deliberately set about finding a husband for her. And when they have found some one, who by birth, fortune, or other qualifications is considered a suitable mate, the 'jeune fille' is brought from the convent where she has been trained by unworldly women for a life in the world, and the two are formally betrothed."

Lacking the frills and formalities of their Eastern counterparts, this illustration by Matt Clark (1903-1972) is titled "Wedding Scene." Gouache on Board, it was reproduced in a 1949 issue of *American Weekly.*
Photograph courtesy Alan M. Goffman, American Illustration

Clearly the "Roaring Twenties" afforded the convent-bred French bride little of the emancipation being sporadically enjoyed by her "sisters" abroad. Not only was her life's mate chosen without her consideration, but after marriage she also abdicated many of her legal rights, for freedom from the convent brought many restrictions in marriage, one of which stipulated that she could not cross the French border—not even into neighboring Switzerland—without written permission from her husband. Compounding her demeaned state, her signature had no legal validity, the only recognized one now being solely that of her husband.

"The meeting."

ROMANCE IN THE REGENCY, VICTORIAN, AND EDWARDIAN PERIODS

"Courtship consists of a number of quiet attentions, none so pointed as to alarm, nor so vague as not to be understood."

Shakespeare

"It is easier to be a lover than a husband for the simple reason that it is more difficult to be witty every day than to say pretty things from time to time."

Honore de Balzac

A "courting tool" in Victorian times. "Spinning Yarn" by Anna Whelan Betts, circa 1915, was probably a book illustration.

Photograph courtesy Alan M. Goffman, American Illustration

Where society and social climate permitted, romance blossomed throughout the nineteenth century, first in the more constrained atmosphere of the Regency and Victorian eras, and from there into the flowery and sentimental Edwardian period of the twentieth century. Courtship became an art form for which all men could but hope (with trepidation) to be prepared and for which most women held nothing but the highest of expectations. Protocol was everything, manners in wide-ranging areas of social discourse were rigid. Paper and pen assumed great importance, as the thoughts and romantic aspirations—in none but the purest and most restrained form—were communicated between males and females. It was a courtship dance rarely if ever equalled for its elegance of expression. In tandem, all were representative of a truly "romantic era."

There were, nonetheless, many constraints to impede the path of romance. An 1850 book, *The Lover's Companion, A Handbook of Courtship and Marriage* offered very succinct advice to all who chose to venture through these socially "booby-trapped" waters. A young man who wished to write or even speak to a girl was first expected to get parental permission to "address her." Above all, it was advised, familiarity did indeed breed contempt, and the

33

gentleman was also cautioned to make his visits short—and few and far between. Suitors were advised to proceed cautiously, for to toy with a young lady's affections placed one in the odious category of "cad." This wasn't the only derogatory term with which he was tarred, for such fellows were also called "danglers" and considered beneath contempt.

Familiarity was *verboten,* and to flaunt one's courtship in front of others was viewed as a tasteless display of bad manners. As the *Companion* advised, "Lovers would do well to remember that while courtship is the most absorbing of all occupations *to them,* it is the most insipid, and when too manifest, the most distasteful to others."[1] Guidelines for young ladies were rigid. In *Young Lady's Friends* by Mrs. Farrar she quoted the rules laid down by one Mrs. Sigourney for insuring propriety, advising ". . . young girls to remember that it was for eternity they were preparing and therefore they should not take up all their thoughts with love and marriage . . . . Do not suffer your hand to be held or squeezed, without showing that it displeases you by instantly withdrawing it . . . ."[2]

Such advice resulted in the following rather calamitous observation:

"Some cause, possibly climatic, has certainly reduced the intensity of sex emotion . . . . Perhaps the independence of girlhood makes for a certain hardness instead of a strength of character; perhaps living on the surface of their impractical superficial existence before marriage has precluded any deeper appreciation of emotion, and makes the selection of a life partner more of a cotillion feature than the cataclysmic decision with which she is credited."[3]

> *"What is now called the nature of woman is an eminently artificial thing."*
>
> John Stuart Mill, 1861

"Preparing for the courting."

A shy suitor.

Flying in the face of deeply entrenched Old World societal protocol, the *melting pot* that became America was unique, creating a merging of marriage rituals not found elsewhere. By the close of the nineteenth century, most American women had considerably more freedom in love and courtship than their European counterparts, and throughout much of Victorian middle class society she was left to her own devices in searching for a husband. This was not always an easy task, especially if the young lady lived in a larger city, where socially acceptable opportunities were limited primarily to church groups. These impediments were balanced by the emerging acceptability of the values of love, compatibility, and personal choice as desirable qualities in forging a happy and lasting marriage.

Nonetheless, the majority of Victorian society's elite remained enured in social protocol. Here, engagements often lasted as long as two years, while both males and females were subjected to an investigation into just about every aspect of their lives (and those of their ancestors!).

> *"There is nothing half so sweet in life as love's young dream."*
>
> Moore

All a-twitter, a nosey procession follows the now betrothed couple after the announcement at Sunday services of their impending marriage.

The Paradise Covered Bridge.   *Illustration by G. Robert Wagner of Lancaster County Recreations.*

Her carriage awaits! This circa 1900 wedding dress features handmade lace and a bodice embellished with pearls on front and sleeves. The veil of Belgian lace, circa 1910-1920, features a headpiece decorated with French wax flowers and embroidered with pearls and beads. Fashioned by hand, a Battenberg lace coat, lined with silk and festooned with silk passementarie and tassels, along with a hand-embroidered batiste parasol, circa 1900, completes this delightfully elegant ensemble from a bygone era.
Courtesy Jana Starr Antiques.
Model: Michele Mathewson

The more prominent in American and European society, the deeper they delved . . . money, inner-circle connections, family lineage. Once the betrothal finally took place (if indeed it did!) any previous disagreements disappeared. " . . . the couple was feted publicly, nourished privately, and their mutual fortunes advanced in every possible way. To their delight, the lovers could now stroll alone, hold hands, even go off during the day for a carriage ride unchaperoned."[4] From the so-called "upper" classes to those of rural America, the covered bridge—one of today's architectural treasures—became an eager suitor's delight. Shielded from prying eyes, he could steal a kiss or two as the carriage or horse and buggy passed through—obviously, the longer the bridge, the better!

During the Victorian era, as with other groups throughout history that were obsessed with outward amenities and social correctness (as well as impressing others in their insular society), much was made of wedding-related events before and after the ceremony. In

"The thousand dollar table," *The Designer,* 1913

the April 1913 issue of *The Designer* magazine, a wedding breakfast table, seating eight, is illustrated. Called "the thousand dollar table" it featured cut-work embroidery trailing around the tablecloth, silver deposit glassware, glittering crystal candelabrum, and French bisque ladies with light shining through their electrified lamps. We are told that these cost a whopping $20 each, a tidy sum for 1913—a collector's dream some seven decades later!

Middle class America was primarily responsible for forging new ground in the "mating dance." Not only had the value of personal feelings come to the fore, but even as early as the late 1800s, women were encouraged to give consideration to furthering their education and delaying marriage. These were bold, new ideas and they laid the groundwork not only for increased freedom in marriage but widening opportunities for women in everyday endeavors. As might be expected, opposing voices were quick to express displeasure. The role of a young lady in preparation for her forthcoming adult and marital life was clearly and frighteningly defined when a Victorian clergyman made this doleful observation . . . "Must we crowd education on our daughters, and for the sake of having them 'intellectual,' make them puny, nervous, and their whole earthly existence a struggle between life and death?"5

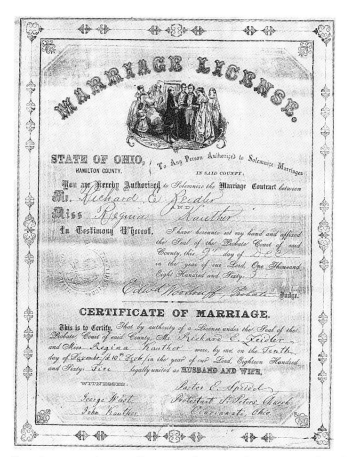

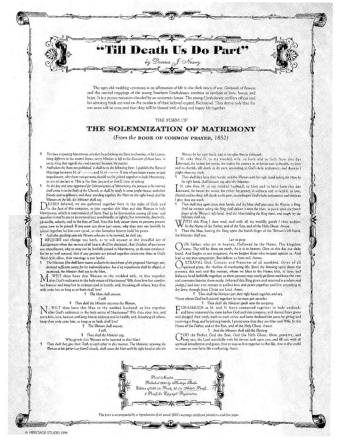

Two vintage marriage certificates one from Hamilton County, Ohio, dated 1865 *(top and left)* and *The Solemnization of Matrimony* from the *Book of Common Prayer,* 1852 *(right).*

Courtesy collection of D. J. Neary

The 1897 wedding of May Churchill and George Talcott of New Britain, Connecticut.

Photograph courtesy of The Connecticut Historical Society, Hartford, Connecticut

From the period 1893 to 1899, this DeLameter and Son photograph is of Jennie P. Allen and her unidentified groom . . . a Victorian gentleman with starched collar, long waistcoat, gloves, and the center-parted hair and moustache so *de rigeur* for the "Gay Nineties" male.

Photograph courtesy of The Connecticut Historical Society, Hartford, Connecticut

A wedding party from the early 1900s (most probably circa 1910-1918). Note tiered peplum gowns.

Photograph courtesy The Connecticut Historical Society, Hartford, Connecticut

Wedding photograph of Theodate Pope, who was then 49 years old, and John Wallace Riddle.
Photograph courtesy of The Hill-Stead Museum Archives, Farmington, Connecticut

Departing from the generally accepted role of women during the Victorian era, the story of one Victorian woman is a stunning repudiation of this clergyman's dour appraisal. Her name was Theodate Pope, and she was born in 1867 in Cleveland, Ohio, the only child of an iron industrialist and his wife. She attended the exclusive Miss Porter's School in Farmington, Connecticut, and was encouraged as a free thinker by her parents, her life not molding to those of her Victorian peers. An early breaking from tradition occurred when one of her beaus was invited to accompany the Pope family on an around-the-world tour, during which the couple was permitted the unthinkable for a duo not yet betrothed—at least by the most rigid of Victorian social standards—for they frequently spent afternoons touring the streets of foreign cities unchaperoned. Theodate went on to become a personage in her own right. One of America's first female architects, she opened offices in New York City in 1913.

As had many of her life's goals, Theodate's view of marriage defied those of Victorian tradition. She didn't take a husband until the age of 49, her choice being career diplomat, John Wallace Riddle. One of Riddle's female cousins wrote an amusing letter to Theodate when the engagement was announced. In part, it read, "My theory has always been that one ought to marry for a good disposition rather than for love as safer for one's happiness . . . and when you add to that a delightful sense of humor what more could we ask! . . . and think of being made love to in nine different languages!"[6]

Typifying the Victorian wedding of 1900, the bridal party for the marriage of Theodate Pope's cousin Elizabeth Brooks of Salem, Ohio and Fred Emery pose in front of the enormous reception tent and at the bridal table inside.
Photographs courtesy of The Hill-Stead Museum Archives, Farmington, Connecticut

Following Theodate's marriage, a male Riddle cousin relayed this account of the wedding: "We all gathered in the dining room and sitting room and outside, as we felt inclined. Then Theo and John Riddle came walking down the lane, he having . . . met Theo at the steps at the upper end. . . . Theo carrying a bouquet of lillies of the valley which he had given her. . . . While passing through the sitting room and seeing us all standing expectantly lined up, she said with her rare smile, 'Oh, is it time?' . . . [and] motioned to the people in the back . . . saying, 'Come nearer, nearer.' " When the couple departed after the ceremony, she made the same gesture to the schoolgirls from Miss Porters who were assembled outside, saying " '. . . I want to ask you to remember us in your prayers, not that we may be happy but that it may be well with us. . . . May God's blessing be upon all of you here, and I think a happy bride's prayer will be in Heaven!' "[7]

Theodate Pope-Riddle's will specified that the home built by her parents in Farmington, Connecticut, Hill-Stead, be converted to a museum for the public to enjoy and appreciate. Each room remains as it was when the Pope and Riddle families occupied it, including the priceless works of art they so treasured. The house stands as a tribute to a well-loved Victorian home . . . and a young woman who chose to pursue her own path against the prickly obstacles of staid Victorian traditions.

Circa 1888—Mrs. Charles E. Perkins is seated, as her daughter Emily, in wedding finery, gazes pensively out the window.

Photograph courtesy The Connecticut Historical Society, Hartford, Connecticut

Observations of the Literati . . .
Samuel Clemens (Mark Twain);
Harriet Beecher Stowe;
Jane Austen; and Charlotte Bronte

Literary works and personal observations provide invaluable insight into the social mores of the past. In fiction lies fact, and readers of today become privy to vivid word pictures that allow them to enter the worlds of yesteryear as silent observers. For here one uncovers not only descriptions of the visible accoutrements of daily life but the author's keen insights, as well.

Samuel L. Clemens (Mark Twain) (1835-1910)

"Love is a madness; if thwarted, it develops fast." . . . *The Memorable Assassination,* an essay by Mark Twain.

The writings of Mark Twain need little introduction. However, in lesser-known works titled *Adam's Diary* and *Eve's Diary,* Clemens gave the age-old mystery of the differences between males and females and their views on mating, love, and marriage a satirical, insightful "twist" . . . traveling to the time of Earth's Biblical first inhabitants, Adam and Eve. Although written in Victorian times, it reflects not only his observations as they relate to that period but also those of countless befuddled ladies and gentlemen from centuries long past. Even today, Twain's contrast between Adam and Eve is an amusing excursion into the often puzzling differences between the sexes . . . which he seems to have sorted out quite succinctly!

Samuel L. Clemens, always one to defy convention and step out of the "mainstream," is bedecked in his honorary doctorate garb for daughter Clara's 1909 wedding to Ossip Gabrilowitsch. Clemens is at the left. Others pictured, from left to right are: Jervis Langdon, Jean Clemens (Clemens' daughter), Ossip Gabriolowitsch, Clara Clemens Gabrilowitsch, and the Reverend Joseph Twichell.

Excerpts from *Adam's Diary:*

"The new creature says its name is Eve. . . . It says it is not an It, it is a She. This is probably doubtful; yet it is all one to me; what she is were nothing to me if she would but go by herself and not talk."

"I escaped last Tuesday night and travelled two days, and built me another shelter, in a secluded place, and obliterated my tracks as well as I could, but she hunted me out. . . . I was obliged to return with her, but will presently emigrate again, when occasion offers."

"She fell in the pond yesterday, when she was looking at herself in it, which she is always doing."

"She has taken up with a snake now. The other animals are glad, for she was always experimenting with them and bothering them; and I am glad, because the snake talks, and this enables me to get a rest."

"She says the snake advises her to try the fruit of that tree, and says the result will be a great and fine and noble education. I told her there would be another result too—it would introduce death into the world. . . . I advised her to keep away from the tree. She said she wouldn't. I foresee trouble. Will emigrate."

"Perhaps I ought to remember that she is very young, a mere girl, and make allowances. . . she can't speak for delight when she finds a new flower, she must pet it and caress it and smell it and talk to it, and pour out endearing names upon it. And she is color-mad: brown rocks, yellow sand, gray moss, blue sky. . . . If she could quiet down and keep still a couple of minutes at a time, it would be a reposeful spectacle. In that case I think I could enjoy looking at her . . . for I am come to realize that she is a quite remarkably comely creature. . . . I recognized that she was beautiful."

"I found this place, outside the Park, and was fairly comfortable for a few days, but she found me out. . . . In fact, I was not sorry she came, for there are but meager pickings here and she brought some of those apples. I was obliged to eat them. I was so hungry. It was against my principles, but I find that principles have no real force except when one is well fed. . . . She came curtained in boughs and bunches of leaves, and when I asked her what she meant by such nonsense, and snatched them away and threw them down, she tittered

and blushed. I had never seen a person titter and blush before, and to me it seemed unbecoming and idiotic. Hungry as I was, I laid down the apple half eaten . . . and arrayed myself in the discarded boughs and branches. . . . I find that she is a good deal of a companion. I see I should be lonesome and depressed without her, now that I have lost my property. Another thing, she says it is ordered that we work for our living hereafter. She will be useful. I will superintend."

Excerpts from *Eve's Diary:*

" . . . I already begin to realize that the core and center of my nature is love of the beautiful . . . and that it would not be safe to trust me with a moon that belonged to another person and that person didn't know I had it. . . . For I do love moons, they are so pretty and so romantic. I wish we had five or six; I would never go to bed; I should never get tired lying on the mossbank and looking up at them. . . . Stars are good, too. I wish I could get some to put in my hair. . . .When they first showed last night, I tried to knock some down with a pole, but it didn't reach, which astonished me. . . . So I cried a little, which was natural I suppose, for one of my age."

"I followed the other Experiment around yesterday afternoon, at a distance, to see what it might be for, if I could. But I was not able to make out. I think it is a man. I had never seen a man, but it looked like one, and I feel sure that that is what it is. . . . It has no hips; it tapers like a carrot; when it stands, it spreads itself apart like a derrick; so I think it is a reptile, though it may be architecture."

"I got it up the tree again. It is up there yet. Resting, apparently. . . . It looks to me like a creature that is more interested in resting than in anything else. It would tire me to rest so much. It tires me just to sit around and watch the tree. I do wonder what it is for; I never see it do anything."

"They returned the moon last night, and I was so happy. . . . I wish I could do something to show my appreciation. I would like to send them some stars, for we have more than we can use. I mean I, not we, for I can see that the reptile cares nothing for such things. . . . It has low tastes, and is not kind."

"When I found it could talk, I felt a new interest in it, for I love to talk; I talk all day, and in my sleep, too, and I am very interesting, but if I had another to talk to I could be twice as interesting, and would never stop, if desired."

"If this reptile is a man, it isn't an *it,* is it? That wouldn't be grammatical, would it? I think it would be *he.* I think so. In that case one would parse it thus: nominative, *he;* dative, *him;* possessive, *his'n.* Well, I will consider it a man and call it he until it turns out to be something else."

"All this week I tagged around after him and tried to get acquainted. I had to do the talking, because he was shy. . . . He seemed pleased to have me around, and I used the sociable 'we' a good deal, because it seemed to flatter him to be included."

"We are getting along very well indeed, now, and getting better and better acquainted. He does not try to avoid me any more, which is a good sign, and shows that he likes to have me with him. During the last day or two I have taken all the work of naming things off his hands, and this has been a great relief to him, for he has no gift in that line, and is evidently very grateful. He can't think of a rational name to save him, but I do not let him see that I am aware of his defect. . . . In this way I have saved him many embarrassments. I have no defect like his."

"My first sorrow. Yesterday he avoided me and seemed to wish I would not talk to him. I could not believe it, and thought there was some mistake, for I loved to be with him, and loved to hear him talk, and so how could it be that he could feel unkind towards me when I had not done anything?"

"I tried to get him some of those apples, but I cannot learn to throw straight. I failed, but I think the good intention pleased him. They are forbidden, and he says I shall come to harm; but so I come to harm through pleasing him, why shall I care for that harm?"

"He talks very little. Perhaps it is because he is not bright, and is sensitive about it and wishes to conceal it. It is a pity that he should feel so, for brightness is nothing; it is in the heart that the values lie. I wish I could make him understand that a loving good heart is riches, and riches enough, and that without it intellect is poverty."

"No he had no interest in my name. I tried to hide my disappointment, but I suppose I did not succeed. I went away and sat on the moss bank with my feet in the water. It is where I go when I hunger for companionship, some one to look at, some one to talk to. It is not enough—that lovely white body painted there in the pool—but it is something, and something is better than utter loneliness."

"All the morning I was at work improving the estate; and I purposely kept away from him in the hope that he would get lonely and come. But he did not. At noon I stopped for the day and took my recreation by flitting all about with the bees and the butterflies and revelling in the flowers. . . . I gathered them and made them into wreaths and garlands and clothed myself in them while I ate my luncheon—apples . . . then I sat in the shade and wished and waited. But he did not come. But no matter. Nothing would have come of it, for he does not care for flowers. He calls them rubbish and cannot tell one from another. . . . He does not care for me, he does not care for flowers . . . is there anything he does care for, except building shacks to coop himself up in from the good clean rain, and thumping the melons, and sampling the grapes, and fingering the fruit on the trees, to see how those properties are coming along?"

An early postcard showing a cherubic Eve by Grace Drayton.
Courtesy Susan Brown Nicholson

"When I look back, the Garden is a dream to me. It was beautiful . . . but now it is lost, and I shall not see it any more. The Garden is lost, but I have found *him*, and am content. He loves me as well as he can; I love him with all the strength of my passionate nature, and this, I think, is proper to my youth and sex. . . .

Yes, I think I love him merely because he is *mine* and is *masculine*. There is no other reason, I suppose. And so I think it is as I first said: that this kind of love is not a product of reasonings and statistics. It just *comes*—none knows whence—and cannot explain itself. And doesn't need to. It is what I think. But I am only a girl, and the first that has examined this matter, and it may turn out that in my ignorance and inexperience I have not got it right."

These excerpts from the Adam and Eve diaries are by permission of Richard A. Watson and Chemical Bank as trustees of the Mark Twain Foundation.

Not one to limit his sharp wit to his writings, Samuel Clemens' inclinations couldn't be controlled, even when expressing his intentions toward Olivia Langdon. "After Samuel Clemens had proposed to Miss Olivia Langdon and been accepted, he came to the most difficult part of his task, to address her father. 'Judge,' he said to the dignified millionaire, 'have you seen anything going on between your daughter and me?' 'What? What?' exclaimed the judge rather sharply, apparently not understanding the situation yet doubtless getting a glimpse of it from the inquiry. 'Have you seen anything going on between Olivia and me?' 'No, no, indeed!' replied the magnate sternly, 'No, sir, I have not.' [To which Clemens replied] 'Well! Look sharp and you will.' "[9]

Later the judge called Clemens into his study. " 'My daughter's welfare is very near to my heart, and before you become engaged I would like to know something more than I do about you. . . . Can you give me the names of any of your friends who can vouch for your steadiness?' 'Sir,' replied Clemens, 'Your sentiments are in every way correct . . . therefore, permit me to give you the names of a few of my friends. They will all lie for me, just as I would for them under a like circumstance.' "[10]

That Twain, for all his rapier wit and keen insights, was a devoted husband and loving father is particularly evident in the writings of his daughter Susy. Susy Clemens, who died tragically in 1896 at the age of twenty-four, began writing a biography of her father when she was thirteen years old. In describing her parents' courtship and marriage, she wrote (in her innocent, childlike manner), "Soon papa [came] back east, and papa and mamma were married. Papa wrote mamma a great many beautiful love letters when he was engaged to mamma, but mamma says I am too young to see them yet; I asked Papa . . . how I could write a Biography of him without his love-letters, papa said that I could write mama's oppinion [sic] of them, and that would do just as well. So I will do as papa says . . . mamma says she thinks they are the loveliest love-letters that were ever written . . . she thinks that Hawthorne's love-letters to Mrs. Hawthorne are far inferior to these."[11]

"After the ceremony," as depicted by Charles Dana Gibson.

"Did you kiss the bride?"
"No, I'm going to wait until they come back from their honeymoon and get settled down."

The Victorian mating dance . . . titled "Cupid's Sting" this gouache on artist board is by Walter Granville Smith, circa 1895, and was possibly a *Truth* magazine illustration.

Photograph courtesy Alan M. Goffman, American Illustration

Of current vintage, this Madame Alexander doll is a depiction of Amy's wedding finery from Louisa May Alcott's *Little Women.*

HARRIET BEECHER STOWE (1811-1896)

Credited as being America's first woman journalist, Harriet Beecher Stowe was a neighbor of Samuel Clemens in what became a conclave of cultural, intellectual, and literary personages known as Nook Farm in Hartford, Connecticut. Stowe made enormous social and societal contributions through her vast body of works, which included the controversial *Uncle Tom's Cabin.* Age was no deterrent to her prolific writing skills, for she penned 22 of her thirty-three books between the ages of 51 and 73!

When the announcement of Harriet Beecher's marriage to Calvin Stowe appeared in the newspapers, her sister Katherine was mistakenly designated as the bride. The resultant confusion was a source of amusement to Harriet, and she wrote the following "tongue in cheek" observation in a letter to the Beecher family shortly after the nuptials. "I suppose

From the Harriet Beecher Stowe Center:

In the summer of 1991, the Harriet Beecher Stowe Center recreated the look of a Victorian household as it made preparations for a family wedding and reception. From parlor to kitchen, the rooms reflected the impending festivities. Presentation tables in the parlors were laden with displays of the wedding gifts. The dining room is ready, with cakes and punch, while in the kitchen a breakfast tray is prepared to take to the bedroom of the bride-to-be.

A sampling of typical nineteenth century wedding gifts includes (clockwise from left): on top of a silver tray, matching ladle and forks, damask table linens, opera glasses, a mosaic brooch, handkerchief ring; Tiffany bud vase, porcelain vase, a set of six silver coffee spoons with matching sugar tongs, a carriage clock case; mother-of-pearl inlaid box, ceramic bureau tray, and a book.
Photograph by Beverly J. Zell, courtesy of the Harriet Beecher Stowe Center, Hartford, Connecticut

In Mrs. Stowe's bedroom, a formal gown of golden brocade and white kid leather shoes await. The gown has a full train and separate yellow satin skirt. Accessories included a beaded purse, a lightweight shawl, and an ostrich feather fan mounted on ivory sticks.
Photograph by Beverly J. Zell, courtesy of the Harriet Beecher Stowe Center, Hartford, Connecticut

Two early twentieth century gowns indicative of the styles of the era. On the left, circa 1907, one of silk crepe with Val lace inserts and train, appropriate for wear by a guest or even the mother-of-the-bride; on the right, a gown of cream-colored crocheted Irish lace over a pale peach ruffled petticoat and taffeta lining with an elaborate train. Circa 1905, it could have been worn as a bridal gown.
Photograph courtesy Helen Winter Associates

This pale blue taffeta brocade gown with black velvet trim, circa 1905, would have been appropriate for either the mother of the bride or an attendant.
Photograph courtesy Helen Winter Associates

Dating from the late nineteenth century, this sage green faille gown, trimmed with peach and silver brocade could possibly have been worn by a mother-of-the-bride. Note the ruffled train.
Photograph courtesy Helen Winter Associates

you have all heard that Kate and I have been pitted against each other in the newspapers as to who should have Mr. Stowe to husband—but I desire to [tell] all people to wit that he married *me*—whether he married her too or not is no concern of mine—he doesn't seem to remember whether he did or not."[12]

In 1853, some seventeen years after her marriage, Harriet Beecher Stowe wrote to a friend about those early years. "I was married when I was twenty-five years old to a man rich in Greek and Hebrew, Latin and Arabic and alas! rich in nothing else. When I went into housekeeping my entire stock of china for parlor and kitchen was bought for eleven dollars . . . [Later] I found . . . that I had neither plates nor teacups to set a table for my father's family . . . I thought it best to reinforce the establishment by getting me a tea-set that cost ten dollars more, and this, I believe, formed my whole stock in trade for some years."[13]

Calvin Stowe also had a "way with words," penning these intense sentiments to Harriet Beecher prior to their marriage. "I wish once in a while that you might be able to look into my soul and see for yourself the exact *form* and *dimensions* of my feelings toward you. . . . I have . . . a feeling of *irreparableness*, as though my blood somehow circulated through your veins, and if you were torn from me I should *bleed to death*."[14]

Although devoted to each other, their differing personalities were a source of conflict, and Calvin's written comments took on a somewhat sharper edge, as in this later excerpt from a note to Harriet: "Permanency is my delight; yours everlasting change . . . I am naturally particular, you are naturally slack." As further explained by William Peterson in his book *Harriet Beecher Stowe Had a Husband*, "He was the penny-pincher, who felt every luxury would be a step toward the poorhouse; she, the visionary who always had a fresh dream to replace an old one that had gone sour." Inept and lacking in physical dexterity, Calvin was of little, if any, assistance with household repairs and the necessities of everyday life, for, as Peterson notes, "Harriet is said to have prayed, 'Lord, don't take me until my dear husband is gone, for nobody else can do for him what I can.'"

Ann Shapiro also observes the following in *Unlikely Heroines: Nineteenth-Century American Women Writers and the Woman Question*, "For Stowe marriage was sacred, and she was sharply critical of men as well as women who failed to live up to their marital obligations, even advocating a woman's right to divorce in extreme cases." It seems obvious that, although an early proponent of women's rights, Stowe was adamant in her belief that women's domestic duties were of equal importance to those of the male, and that she had a duty and obligation to fulfill them.

Stowe wasn't reluctant to express her harsh criticism of the behavior of Lord Byron toward his wife, and expounded on these views in a magazine article published by *Atlantic Monthly* in 1869 and later expanded into a book, *Lady Byron Vindicated*. In it, she "suggests that the marriage [to Lord Byron] should have been dissolved . . ." Stowe wrote passionately about the Byron case: "man may wallow in filth like the swine, may turn his home into a hell,

Often referred to as a Victorian vamp, Ada Menken (mid-1830s-1868) was a talented actress and poetess, attracting numerous renowned suitors. She also flew in the face of conventional female expectations when she wrote, "Daughters should be trained with higher and holier motives than that of being fashionable and securing wealthy husbands . . . there are other missions for women than that of wife and mother." Married and divorced four times, Menken added, "I believe all good men should be married. Yet I don't believe in women being married. Somehow they all sink into nonentities after this epoch in their existence."[15]

Valuing the proper expression of the written word, (a skill that many honed to perfection), in addition to letter-writing, many Edwardian and Victorian ladies faithfully made detailed entries in their small, leather-bound, personal diaries.

beat and torture his children, forsake the marriage-bed for four rivals yet all this does not dissolve the marriage bed on her part . . ."

As described in her highly acclaimed biography, *Harriet Beecher Stowe: A Life,* Joan Hedrick observes that "Unlike the male-dominated marriages of the eighteenth century, Calvin and Harriet's union was a 'companionate marriage'. . . . Underlying the companionate marriage was a commitment to the autonomy and personhood of woman that would have been unheard of in the eighteenth century." Indeed, Harriet Beecher Stowe was not only a pioneer in her writings but also in her views of marriage and the intermeshing goals of both sexes in the union.

Jane Austen (1776-1817)

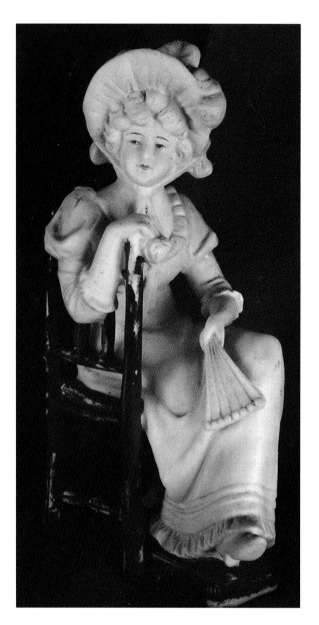

Jane Austen's insightful portrayals of life during the late eighteenth century and early nineteenth are of as much, if not more, interest to audiences today than when they first appeared. Each work masterfully combines comedic observations with strong, sometimes romantic, characterizations.

Although the details are shrouded in contradictions, it appears that Jane was plagued by an early, short-lived, but meaningful attachment that prematurely ended in tragedy. Apparently, while touring Devonshire in 1801, the family met a young man (in one version a clergyman, in another a naval officer) who captured Jane's heart and charmed her family—so much so, in fact, that they "invited him to join them at a later stage on their tour. But instead of his arrival, a letter was received announcing his death."[16]

Even though she attracted numerous admirers, that the memory of the gentleman she met in 1801 was still embedded in her heart is apparent in a note to her niece Fanny many years later. In it she wrote "You like him well enough to marry but not well enough to wait . . . nothing can be compared to the misery of being bound *without* love, bound to one, and preferring another."[17] If such was the case it undoubtedly influenced the characterizations in her writings. "She [Jane Austen] was discovering already the truth she was to state so poignantly in her last novel, *Persuasion,* namely that women have a sad ability to go on loving when hope is gone."[18]

In 1802, Jane was betrothed to Harris Bigg-Wither, a gentleman six years younger than she and brother to three of her closest friends. Although his social standing and finances would ensure security for Jane and her family, the engagement was short-lived. After only one sleepless night, she decided that the commitment made the day before had been a mistake! Her strongly-held views on love and marriage are solidified by Lord David Cecil's observation that "Her actual opinion of them has not altered; she still holds the view that love should be a 'rational' passion, inseparable from esteem and respect for the character of the person loved. . . . She has grown aware that marriage without love all too often leads to love without marriage."[19] It is most probably for these reasons that Jane Austen never married.

> ❧ *"She'll wish there was more, and that's the great art o' letter-writin'.
> . . . "* Charles Dickens, Pickwick Papers (1836-37)
>
> ❧ *The days of comforably established Regency, Vicatorian and
> Edwardian married women were much the same, consisting of let-
> ter-writing (in which they took much pride), planning menus, dis-
> cussing household assignments with the servants, and keeping house-
> hold ledger accounts. When these activities were completed, there were
> walks, music lessons, carriage rides, social visits, and charitable
> endeavors.*

Herewith, some observations on courtship and marriage during this period, as well as excerpts from Jane Austen's writings:

Jane wrote again to Fanny about Fanny's confusion as to whether to accept a suitor's proposal of marriage: ". . . the more I write about him, the warmer my feelings become, the more strongly I feel the sterling worth of such a young Man and the desirableness of your growing in love with him again. I recommend this most thoroughly." But later she continued, "And now, my dear Fanny, having written so much on one side of the question, I shall turn round and entreat you not to commit yourself further, and not to think of accepting him unless you really do like him. Anything is to be preferred or endured rather than marrying without Affection; and if his deficiencies of Manner . . . strike you more than all his good qualities, if you continue to think strongly of them, give him up at once."[20]

The ritual of "coming out" marked a young lady's formal entrance into society. Even this was subject to the family "pecking order," for if an older sister had not yet become

"I've had fully a dozen offers of marriage lately."
"Mercy me! Good ones?"
"Yes. All from George."

Three Victorian ladies "tell it like it is" in this satirical offering by Charles Dana Gibson, circa 1895.

engaged, the younger might have to simply "wait her turn." These convoluted societal protocols were cause for much speculation. In Jane Austen's *Mansfield Park*, Mary Crawford expresses some confusion over Fanny Price's arrangement with society: "Pray is she out, or is she not?—I am puzzled—She dined at the Parsonage with the rest of you, which seemed like being *out:* and yet she says so little that I can hardly suppose she is!"[21]

"It is a truth universally acknowledged that a single man in possession of a good fortune must be in want of a wife." *Pride and Prejudice* (1813)

"Single women have a dreadful propensity to be poor."[22]

Weddings were generally simple and without austentation during Jane Austen's time. "The garments worn at weddings were as various then as now. The wedding of Miss Woodhouse and Mr. Knightley *(Emma)* 'was very much like other weddings where the parties have no taste for finery or parade,' which Mrs. Elton found rather dull: 'very little white satin, very few lace veils, a most pitiful business.' "[23]

Honeymoons were not yet in vogue, and often a sister or female friend accompanied the newlyweds when they departed the church for their new abode . . . and made herself at home for a long visit when they arrived! Reinforcing the validity of this somewhat bizarre practice, in Jane Austen's *Mansfield Park*, Maria "takes her sister with her, and in *Sense and Sensibility*, Mrs. Jennings blames Lucy Steele for being so unkind as to leave her sister behind when she marries Robert Ferrars."[24]

"A woman, especially if she have the misfortune of knowing anything should conceal it as well she can." *Northanger Abbey*, Jane Austen.

A bride and her father approach the altar—as depicted by Charles Dana Gibson.

> 🐚 *Throughout much of the social strata in Victorian times, a young lad had only to attain the age of fourteen and his bride twelve to negate the need for parental permission.*

> 🐚 *Rebellion and an independent attitude aren't solely the domain of the twentieth-century woman, for "In the 1880's the* Chicago Tribune *complained that there were ten thousand homes in Chicago with daughters ignorant 'of the simplest kind of household duties' and that these girls, far from being ashamed of their ignorance, seemed to show no desire to learn."[25]*

Following the marriage of the hero and heroine in *Northanger Abbey,* "Jane Austen avoids the insipidity of a conventional happy ending by pointing out, with demure amusement, that the hero would not have fallen in love with the heroine had he not happened to notice that she was in love with him."[26]

CHARLOTTE BRONTE (1816-1855)

That Charlotte Bronte was blessed with genius is evident early on, for from the age of ten she was writing tales and even completing them in book form, each of which was handsewn and meticulously laid out. Although but a child, her romantic nature was also evident, for "In a profusion of stories which Charlotte made into miniature books, every man is plotting, every woman is waiting—adorned with feathers and properly equipped with ivory fans."[27]

By age twelve Charlotte was convinced that she would never marry, preferring instead to pursue her writing . . . yet another indication that during this time many women of special talent (and even the youthful Charlotte) felt the combination of marriage and a striving toward personal fulfillment would be, at best, difficult—and most likely impossible. Years later her views on marriage and the role of each partner in the union were still of concern, as expressed here in an 1854 letter to a friend: "I think those married women who indiscriminately urge their acquaintance to marry—much to blame. . . . Indeed . . . it is a solemn and strange and perilous thing for a woman to become a wife. Man's lot is far-far different."[28]

That man's lot was indeed viewed as "far-far different" is evident in the fact that *Jane Eyre,* pubished in 1847, was originally written under the pseudonym Currer Bell, as were the writings of her two sisters—Anne known as Acton Bell, and Emily as Ellis Bell. For quite some time, Charlotte's distinguished publisher, George Smith, was also unaware of the true identity of the author of *Jane Eyre.* The mystery caused much speculation among critics as to whether it was penned by a man or a woman and, in some cases, their critiques offered one conclusion if the anonymous writer was a male and another if female—the latter being generally more critical.

Charlotte's life was not without unrequited love and proposals she chose not to accept (by age twenty-five she had received two). For two years, she and her sister Anne studied, with a goal toward teaching, at the school of Constantin Heger in Brussels, and Charlotte returned there a year later to teach. Although Heger was married, Charlotte was infatuated with him, and he, by seductive nuances, did little to discourage her. The romantic attach-

"In his younger days a man dreams of possessing the heart of a woman whom he loves; later, the feeling that he possesses the heart of a woman may be enough to make him fall in love with her."29

Marcel Proust,
*Remembrance of Things Past,
Swan's Way* (1913)

ment appears to have been "in her mind and heart" only. Nevertheless, as with many who have experienced an unreturned attraction, the depth of Bronte's feelings were poignantly expressed through the heroines of her novels, most especially in *Villette.*

In 1854, at age 38, Charlotte married her father's curate, Arthur Bell Nicholls—sadly, only one year before her untimely death in March 1855. That her short-lived marriage was a fulfilling one, and that she was bonded to Nicholls is made clear in notes written to friends during her illness. They refer to him as a kind husband of whom she felt there was no better, a tender nurse, and of great comfort. She makes clear that her heart was joined to his, and "When her husband prayed for her, she said: 'I am not going to die, am I? God will not separate us, we have been so happy.' "30

In many ways, either by actual events or a striving to achieve her own hopes and dreams, the life of Charlotte Bronte reflected those of her heroines. In discussing *Jane Eyre,* author Lyndall Gordon expounds on

1888

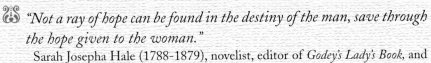

"Not a ray of hope can be found in the destiny of the man, save through the hope given to the woman."
Sarah Josepha Hale (1788-1879), novelist, editor of *Godey's Lady's Book,* and poet responsible for the classic "Mary Had a Little Lamb."

An American handbook of the nineteenth century went so far as to advise the suitor make an unexpected call upon his intended, suggesting that " . . . he will be able thus to form some tolerable estimate of her every-day domestic neatness and habits."31

"I should like to see any kind of a man, distinguishable from a gorilla, that some good and even pretty woman could not shape a husband out of."
Oliver Wendell Holmes, *The Professor at the Breakfast Table.*

"In my youth," said his father, "I took to the law. And argued each case with my wife; And the muscular strength, which it gave to my jaw, Has lasted the rest of my life."

Lewis Carroll, *Alice in Wonderland,* 1865

CAROLINE CRAIG

1896

the nature of the tale. *"Jane Eyre* is above all a pilgrimage. It follows child and woman through pitfalls enroute to her new Eden: a love which unites goodness with the dream of sustained passion."[32] The story of *Jane Eyre*, along with her other literary masterpieces, proved to be part of the lifelong pilgrimage of Charlotte Bronte, as well.

Herewith, some quotes from Charlotte Bronte's *Jane Eyre* (1847):

"The third day from this must be our wedding day, Jane. Never mind fine clothes and jewels now: all that is not worth a fillip." (Edward Rochester to Jane Eyre)

"Mr Rochester, if ever I did a good deed in my life—if ever I thought a good thought—if ever I prayed a sincere and blameless prayer—if ever I wished a righteous wish—I am rewarded now. To be your wife is, for me, to be as happy as I can be on earth." (Jane Eyre to Mr. Rochester)

In reflecting on her happiness after marrying Edward Rochester, Jane wrote, "I hold myself supremely blest—blest beyond what language can express; because I am my husband's life as fully as he is mine."

After receiving a letter from a friend saying that she would give Jane time to rest after the honeymoon before she visited the newlyweds, Mr. Rochester commented, "She had better not wait til then, Jane . . . if she does, she will be too late, for our honey-moon will shine our life-long; its beams will only fade over your grave or mine."

For an unmarried woman of Edwardian times to correspond with a gentleman to whom she was not formally engaged was considered bad form.

Divorce in England during Edwardian times was virtually unheard of, probably because only a wealthy husband could obtain one, and even then it required an Act of Parliament.

"Florence Nightengale, who had both looks and money, also abjured marriage. She believe that her active nature unfitted her for marriage even though her passionate nature impelled her towards it."[33]

With an eye to the Victorian propensity for letter writing, a British manual on the amenities of courtship had some cautionary advice about "placing pen to paper" and ". . . with cool foresight . . . advised against putting anything into a letter that the writer would not want read in court."[33]

Pochoir print features Jean Patou designs for a bride, bridesmaid, and flower girl. Circa 1920-1925.

POMP AND CIRCUMSTANCE

"A wedding is one of the few ceremonies left in modern life (shorn of crusades, royal progressions, and triumphal entries) that lends itself to picturesque pageantry."

Harper's Bazar, May 1922

"The bell in the church tower chimes the hour, a sudden hush falls over the guests who fill the flower-decked pews, the organ peals forth the opening strains of the Lohengrin Wedding March . . . the doors are flung open and a slim-white-robed figure moves slowly up the aisle—the bride of 1928! A murmur of admiration ripples from pew to pew as the procession advances, for all the world loves a bride even more than, according to the old saying, it 'loves a lover.'"

The Delineator, June 1928

By Benito, the "Grand Procession" from a *Le Gazette du Bon Ton* article, circa 1920s, titled *"Du Ridicule Des Corteges et des Remedes a y Porter,"* (Ridiculous Marriage Parades and Remedies for Carrying Them Off).

Some of today's wedding traditions had far different meanings in earlier times—in fact, when it came to bridal colors, "black was white," and "white was black." Indeed, "classic white for the classic bride" wasn't always socially acceptable, and many cultures did not afford it the same aura of chastity and innocence it was later accorded. In fact, white signified death and mourning to the Biblical Jews. . . surely not an "upbeat" state of mind to intrude on one's wedding day!

Processions leading to and from the church assumed almost as much importance as the ceremony itself. In some cultures, color was again significant. Gray was considered lucky for this propitious journey, first in the color of the horses that pulled the carriages and later in the shade of the automobiles that carried the bridal party. The early Normans went one step further, for there the brilliant scarlet of the horses' harnesses became a talisman of sorts . . . it was thought to frighten away witches!

Although the bridal gown has often been chosen with an eye to maintaining social status, in Renaissance France, the groom controlled the outcome. Since the bride's wedding finery was regarded as a significant barometer of his prosperity, many gentlemen financially overextended themselves in order to have gems and pearls encrusted in their intended's gown . . . thus impressing their peers, but at the same time entering the state of matrimony with a back-breaking load of debt.

Steeped in social mores, traditional, bridal attire is a major consideration for brides of most countries, and even specific regions within that country. Some areas in Russia feature elaborate headdresses of flowers and pearls. In Sri Lanka and India the sari, often embroidered in gold, is at the center of importance, as are the diamond and gold baubles, signifying the sun and the moon, that glitter in the bride's hair.

Generally regarded as "the bride's day," history gives clear evidence that the groom was not to be ignored in this parade of fashion and pomp. From the black suits with cream accessories and lace handkerchiefs of the mid-1800s to the more ornate, but nonetheless masculine fashions of later in that century, like high silk hats, waistcoats, gloves and canes

Pochoir print from *Le Gazette du Bon Ton*, pre-1920s.

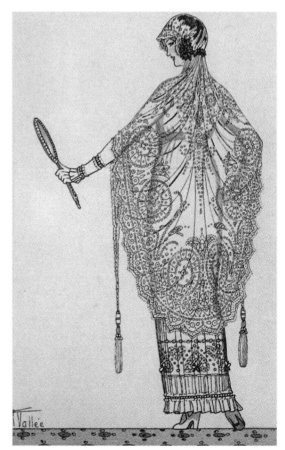

Titled *Une Mariee*, this print of a Venetian lace wedding gown is from *Costumes Parisiens*, dated 1913.

(often all in white), the groom too played a role in wedding protocol and pageantry.

These gentleman could never overtake the *jeunesse doree* during the time of the French Revolution, where wedding finery reflected their normal attire of "... laces, velvets, and shiny high-heeled boots pasted with glittering glass stones like gems."[1] Going back to ancient times, history is replete with societies in which the gentleman "preened his feathers" with as much abandon as the females, often overtaking her in the process. Having garnered his fair share of attention on a daily basis, this "peacock" wasn't about to take a "back seat" on his wedding day.

The extravagance of elaborate weddings during the past few centuries has its roots in ancient traditions. Observing this custom with a jaundiced eye many centuries ago, the Emperor Augustus made a valiant attempt to restrict the amount that could be spent on them ... but to no avail. Such admonitions weren't successful and they surely wouldn't be now, for, as reported in a 1994 article in *U.S.*

From *"For the Well-Dressed Man— How to Dress Properly for the Formal and Informal Wedding"*—Vanity Fair, May 1926:

"... The turnout of the correctly dressed man at a wedding is identical with that worn on any other occasion when formal day dress is required: namely, the top hat, cutaway coat, striped trousers and black calf or patent leather shoes ... his cutaway must be cut along smart lines and fit perfectly and his accessories must be correct in every detail ..."

Twenty years made little difference in what was expected in wedding attire for the fashionably correct gentleman, as attested to in an Esquire *article from the 1940s titled "Guide to Good Grooming":*

"Formal Day Wedding: Oxford grey cutaway coat ... lily of the valley boutonniere, pale grey waistcoat, black and grey striped trousers, white pleated bosom shirt, black and white silk ascot, wing collar, black silk hat, grey mocha gloves, black half-hose, and black straight-tip shoes."

"Formal Evening Wedding: Midnight blue tailcoat with satin lapels, trousers to match, lily of the valley boutonniere, wing collar, white pique butterfly bow tie, white pique starched bosom shirt, pearl studs, white pique waistcoat, black hose, and black patent leather shoes. Black silk hat is correct."

Waiting at the church ... *Vanity Fair,* May 1926.

News and World Report, $35 billion dollars are spent in the United States alone to "join these two in holy matrimony," with the average spent on today's formal wedding a mind-boggling $17,470! When the pocketbook allows (and often when it doesn't), one steeped in pageantry and tradition remains the "wedding of choice" for most bridal couples.

Nevertheless, many contemporary bridal couples have chosen a plethora of unusual spots to "tie the knot"—like atop a Mardi Gras float, or while tumbling through the air tethered to parachutes. Others have preferred historic, but unusual locations. A number of these involved the old covered bridge in Sheffield, Massachusetts, which burned to the ground in 1994. One "bridge" ceremony had only three participants, the gowned bride, the tuxedoed groom, and the Justice of the Peace. In another, the couple shouldn't have been surprised when a lightning storm disrupted the proceedings—the ceremony was held on Friday the 13th! Wedding or no wedding, practicality was an overshadowing concern for another ceremony performed on the same bridge at 6 a.m., thus enabling both the bride and groom to report to their respective jobs on time.

> In Scotland during the last century, the kiss bestowed on the bride in some of their wedding ceremonies qualifies as strange indeed, for it is reported that the groom often held his bride by the ears when he "sealed it with a smooch."

Not to be overlooked in any tale of marriage traditions are elopements, which grew in popularity during the twentieth century. Elopement for many was an impulsive, spur-of-the-moment act. Others simply preferred to forego the "pomp and circumstance" and the expense, while fear of family intervention was undoubtedly a factor in many decisions. In any case, they communicated their intentions to no one—except perhaps a couple invited to accompany them and act as attendants— married in secrecy, and faced the consequences later. The "ladder to the window" scenario, so popular in early films, romanticized the notion and undoubtedly occurred from time to

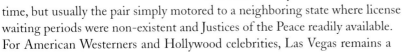

A traditional Chinese wedding couple

time, but usually the pair simply motored to a neighboring state where license waiting periods were non-existent and Justices of the Peace readily available. For American Westerners and Hollywood celebrities, Las Vegas remains a favorite elopement locale. Here a plethora of chapels await, providing quick, no-frills weddings.

Popular during the Victorian era and through the early decades of the twentieth century was the *shivaree* or *charivari*, which good-naturedly spoofed the romantic serenade. When the newlyweds left the church a procession of raucous revelers followed them to their home, beating on pots and pans, setting off firecrackers, and often continuing the good-natured revelry until the lights in the couple's home were turned off. Undoubtledly an offshoot of similar European customs, and even the merrymaking of Elizabethan times, in the United States it was most prominent in the Midwest among the working classes and those in rural areas. The *shivarees* were more rambunctious than the popular practice of tying shoes to the bumpers of newlyweds' cars and the honking of horns in parade-like fashion as guests proceeded to the reception. All, however, had the same purpose—sending the couple into matrimony with a modicum of embarrassment and plenty of noise!

Bridal attire from the period of Louis XVI.

Stunning in white satin and mother of pearl—the bride of 1925.

Harper's Bazar, May 1925

An unusual wedding dress circa early 1900s. The bodice is silk satin; the skirt consists of layers of fine silk Chantilly lace. Both bodice and skirt are decorated with large hand-crafted, silk/satin flowers bordered with burnished gold thread—a look indicative of the Arts and Crafts style of the period.

Courtesy Jana Starr Antiques

From the early 1900s, a layered dress of English net over silk chiffon topping silk charmeuse, the various tiers revealed by successively longer skirts; the top layer is embroidered with glass beads in an Art Nouveau pattern; the high waist is ornamented with a central medallion embroidered with beads and a single large pearl.

Courtesy Jana Starr Antiques

Restrained glitter, shown here in two "silver" wedding gowns . . . the one by Jenny (right) is of silver tissue faille, accented with silver flowers. The other, titled "White Satin and Silver." (above) is by Callot and features silver overlay tastefully covering the massive veil and also parts of the satin skirt. Note the cascade of flowers draped down the front. Both appeared in the May 1926 issue of *Harper's Bazar.*

> In Victorian times, the bride stood on what was called a "sheet island" when she donned the bridal gown and veil, thus avoiding even a hint or dust or dirt to spoil the virginal ensemble.

A Dutch-inspired wedding gown, circa 1920s.

Although from the 1920s, this gown and headdress reflect the Medieval influence.

GIDDING CREATIONS DESIGNED FOR SPRING WEDDINGS &c

POSSESS A SUBTLE SPLENDOR AS INSPIRING AS THE IMPORTANT FUNCTION THEY GRACE

VEILS
BRIDAL GOWNS
BRIDESMAIDS DRESSES
GOWNS FOR MATRONS OF HONOR
TROUSSEAU LINGERIE
RECEPTION COSTUMES
TRAVEL SUITS AND ACCESSORIES

OUR DRESSMAKING & TAILORING SALONS ARE MAKING TO ORDER EVERY INCOMING PARIS FASHION IN THE EXACT DUPLICATE OR YOUR OWN MODIFICATION OF IT.

For wedding apparel, a 1921 advertisement for J. M. Gidding & Co.

For the perfect reception—a 1923 advertisement for Louis Sherry of New York and Paris, and from 1919, another for Dean's of New York City.

The beauty of Cheney Silks from the renowned Cheney Brothers mills, shown here in a 1919 advertisement.

Emily Hathaway, a bride of 1921, was wed in the greenery-bedecked alcove window of her family's Victorian-style New Bedford, Massachusetts home.

A proud father escorts his daughter to the church in this advertisement for the Lozier automobile, circa 1914.

Veiled in the mystery and glamour of exquisite duchesse lace, a bride is more charming than ever. The veil, with its magnificent, deep border, is worn over a severely plain, ivory satin gown with a petal train. The veil, $1200. The gown, $75. From the Bride's Room, sixth floor.

Brides of 1937—from Marshall Field & Co.'s *The Bride's Book.*

A memorable day wasn't solely dependent on the bride's dress. In their 1937 Bride's Book, Marshall Field and Company encouraged the upcoming bride to avail herself of two services offered in their beauty salon. One covered the essentials from "head to foot" with "... a face treatment, manicure and a shampoo, topped-off with a coiffure designed just as you would want it for your wedding veil. And on the day of the wedding an attendant will go out to your house to dress your hair and help the wedding party with any last minute touches to coiffure or manicure. Each of these services is $10." The groom was not forgotten, for the bride was advised by Field's Wedding Bureau that they would "... help him select spats, ties, gloves and collars for the groom and ushers" and to also assist him in any way possible.

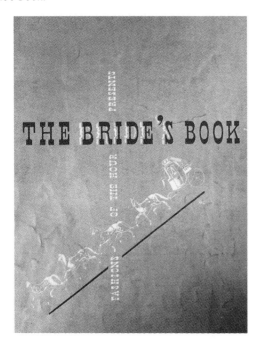

Buttoned and bowed—from the turn-of-the-century, wedding slippers with delicate, white bead embroidery (left).
Courtesy Jana Starr Antiques

Wedding slippers from the 1920s-30s, trimmed with cream and silver brocade and even silver leather (right).
Courtesy Jana Starr Antiques

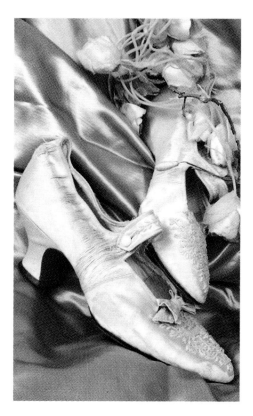

With lacy ruffs and cabbage roses, these hand-decorated bridal shoes also have pearl-beaded heels!
Courtesy Barbra Music Designs

Pale pink slippers for a special bride. Note the hand-sewn clusters of pearl "flowers" and the pearls encircling the heel and vamp.
Courtesy Barbra Music Designs

Romance is in the air . . . and on the feet! Three bridal slippers to make any heart go "pitty-pat."
Courtesy Barbra Music Designs

This silk chiffon dress with intricate tucking and embroidered with pearls, silver, and clear glass beads is dated 1969 and represents the "rich hippie" look of the late '60s and early '70s.
Courtesy Jana Starr Antiques

Perfect for a vintage wedding, this delicated two-piece silk dress from the turn-of-the-century is decorated with handmade lace and silk ribbon. The top is cut like a riding jacket, with a chiffon jabot and cameo embellishing the high neck.
Courtesy Jana Starr Antiques.
Model: Michele Mathewson

A gauntlet to complete the bride's outfit, here in sheer tulle trimmed with delicate beading and flowers.
Courtesy Barbra Music Designs

Beneath the *chupah*.

Photograph courtesy Atlas Floral Decorators, Inc. Photograph by Sarah Merians Photography

Hand-rolled wedding roses.

For today's bride— white kid gloves trimmed with vintage bronze lace.
Courtesy Barbra Music Designs

From bridal parties of the late 1930s-early 1940s, these charming figures served as shower decorations, and are made from papier-mâché, pipe cleaners, and fabric.
Courtesy Jana Starr Antiques

In the April 1939 issue of Vogue, one article featured a soon-to-be young bride, and accompanied her on a search for "just the right" wedding gown and trousseau. The gown finally chosen was of crepe and featured a simple, flowing, softly draped skirt and a long, long train. Its most striking feature, however, was the Deco-look of the pleated bodice that fanned in a delicate spoke-like fashion. The cost: $40. Her hip-length veil topped with a grograin bow could be had for $20. The most expensive item in her trousseau was not the wedding gown, however. It was an all-white silk marquisette long evening dress with a scalloped hem and giant, three-dimension appliqued flowers climbing up one side. The cost: $45!

The bride of 1935. Called the peacock silhouette, and as described in the June 1935 issue of *McCall's*, "It has an uneven hemline—a little short in front, and trailing everywhere else. When the bride walks up the aisle there will be a glimpse of slipper and a flash of ankle. In motion, this is the prettiest slit-at-front skirt in the world."

Wedding attire for the groom. *Esquire* magazine, circa 1941-1945

A symbol of New York's elite society, and the site of many of today's (and yesterday's) wedding receptions, New York City's forty-story Carlyle, which opened in 1930, is a glittering jewel amidst New York's panoramic skyline.

One Carlyle legend recounts how an Upper East Side socialite moved into the hotel while her Park Avenue apartment was being renovated and became so enamored with her suite that when the renovations were completed she sold the apartment and became a permanent resident. Later, two of her children had their wedding receptions there.

Visions in pink—this magnificent cake and the glowing, candlelit ambiance of The Carlyle's Trianon Suite await the bridal party and guests.

Photographs courtesy of The Carlyle.

A JOURNEY THROUGH PERIODICALS OF THE DAY:

The May 1923 issue of Harper's Bazar *described a gown by Patou of "white brocade in straight folds that fall from a pearl and rhinestone-embroidered bodice. . . . It is seen through the faint mist of tulle held closely to the head with white flowers and allowed to fall over the entire gown. The bridesmaid's frock is of two shades of orchid organdy, embroidered with delicate mauve silk flowers."*

"Perhaps the ladies of the Empire wore ivory satin gowns as lovely as this, but it is difficult to believe. The little Empire bodice is outlined by tiny green leaves and pearls; shimmering loops of pearls festoon the gown. Panels of tulle fall from the close tulle head-dress."

Harper's Bazar, *May 1922.*

"The wedding slipper may be of white or silver brocade with a buckle of pearls in a net chou; from Henning."

Vogue, *April 1923.*

In an article titled "The Summer Bride" from the June 1928 issue of Delineator, *were the following descriptions of wedding gowns by premier couturiers of the day:*

"A frock of white taffeta by Lanvin that is Victorian in feeling has a taffeta bodice with yoke and cape of tulle. The skirt has groups of ruffles."

"Madeleine Vionnet's conception of the wedding gown is a sheath of lustrous white crepe satin drawn tightly around the figure and forming a long train."

"Captain Molyneaux caused a sensation when he showed this bridal gown of pale yellow georgette with a long train. The veil is pink tulle."

A mantel for Fall—decorations for pre-wedding dinner in the State Suite of New York's Plaza hotel.
Photograph courtesy Atlas Floral Decorators, Inc.

FANTASY WEDDINGS . . . A ROMANTIC JOURNEY FROM PAST TO PRESENT

Has a particular historical period intrigued you since childhood? Do you sometimes yearn to become a part of that special time, if only for a day? Perhaps you envision yourself presiding over a "Tara-like" setting in the Antebellum South or as a "fair damsel" patiently awaiting your knight in shining armour on the ramparts of a Medieval castle. Are you a frontier gal at heart, fascinated by tales of the Old West, or does your romantic nature draw you to the flowery ambiance of Victorian times?

Take heart, for it's now possible to "live the fantasy"! There are bridal specialists who can assist in replicating a time period of your choice, from historically authentic attire and architectural surroundings to reception details, making the exciting possibilities for a unique "day to remember" virtually limitless.

To follow are modes of wedding attire as assiduously recreated for the modern bride by *Rose D'Zynes*. From beginning to end, the ceremonies and receptions faithfully adhere to the garb and traditions of the chosen period.

Historical background information has been provided by Diane Barr, the founder of *Rose D'Zynes*.

Matrimonial attire reflective of the Spanish Renaissance, here depicting King Phillip II and the Infanta Isabella.

Opposite page: Bridal attire of the English Renaissance.

The Tudor dynasty, which began with Henry VII, marked the end of Medieval costume and a transitional period in fashion. The European Renaissance, which had its beginnings in Italy, followed the Medieval period and covered an approximate one hundred year period between 1450-1550. However, it wasn't until the reign of Queen Elizabeth I (1558-1603) that the Renaissance in England reached full bloom. Along with an open display of jewels and pearls, the figural outline became more slender in style. The look of men was dominated by the Spanish influence, with the sporting of small moustaches and carefully-trimmed beards.

Prior to that time, however, the English Renaissance during the Tudor reigns was less graceful than the Italian and more sober than the German. For men, shoulders were wide and square, dress was shorter, and shoes had square toes. Nonetheless, Henry VIII dazzled his courtiers with ermine-trimmed robes, an abundance of jewels, and codpieces that emphasized his virility. Gentlemen's doublets were open in front, the better to display Spanish blackwork, and the costume often had several pairs of detachable sleeves. English

ladies were inclined to wear black velvet, red silk, and gold brocade, but always with an air of sobriety. The foundation for the skirt was a large hoop, revealing an underskirt of satin or velvet. The neckline was square and low and the sleeves had wide cuffs, sometimes of fur or velvet. It is written that Anne Boleyn wore a nightgown of black satin and velvet, quite possibly the first time the term "nightgown" was used in referring to that article of sleep wear.

In general, the masculine costume of the Renaissance period consisted of a full shirt of linen, which was gathered at the neck and wrists and was edged with fine embroidery in gold, red, or black silk. This embroidery work, which had its origins in Persia, was popular in Spain and became known throughout Europe as Spanish blackwork. The doublet was a short, jacket-like tunic, originally tight but later puffed above the forearm and even

 The Spanish farthing-dale underskirt of the sixteenth century "... consisted of hoops of wire or wood ... The French farthingdale compounded the problem, for the wearer then had to stand inside a ☞

The typical garment of the Medieval period was a loose-fitting tunic, which was worn by both men and women. Changes came slowly, with ladies eventually exerting their more civilized demeanors; garments became close-fitting and revealing, and the tight-fitting sleeves served to emphasize their, hopefully, slender figures. Even the modest damsel revealed at least a portion of her bosom, wearing a kirtle or gown that hugged her closely at the waist and then fell gracefully in long, voluminous folds. It was a time when women

wheel-like contraption with her skirt attached to the rim."[2] In similar fashion, a 1966 bridal gown by the couturier Galanos featured ". . . a raffia mesh cage covered entirely in artificial flowers. Apparently a bride never sits down."[3]

later slashed. Slashing was a style originating among Swiss mercenaries, who stuffed their booty into the "ragged" clothing. The style of this period can still be seen in the Vatican Swiss Guards (attributed to Michaelangelo) and the Beefeaters at the Tower of London, as well as the academic gowns worn at Oxford University. Even the "court cards" in traditional playing cards reflect stylized versions of Renaissance fashion. Shoes had long, pointed toes, and, until around 1510, boots of varying heights were worn.

Special emphasis was placed on embroidery, and when the Oriental steel needle was introduced into Europe by the Moors, embroidery became even finer and more elaborate. In addition, fabrics were decorated in gold, silver, gems, and pearls. Lace was used sparingly, and prior to the seventeenth century generally referred to slender braids and cords that were used as trim or to lace sections of a costume together, although some forms of

were revered in the eyes of the gentlemen, an esteem that elevated courtly wooing to an art form.

Above perhaps all else, a lady's greatest asset was her hair, which was kept alluringly hidden beneath a series of headdresses that grew increasingly elaborate. Medieval brides were "married in their hair," with tresses hanging loose under a caplet of flowers or similar headdress. A brooch was also worn to signify her chastity and the purity of her heart. Sans veil, a square white cloth was held above the wedding couple's heads during the benediction. At the altar, the bride, who stood to her groom's left, placed her right hand on his; however, if she had been widowed or previously married, or even had earlier been betrothed to another, it was customary that the hand be gloved.

For the knight, steeped in ideals of chivalry, clothes served a dual function . . . to attract the attention of the damsel with his dashing figure and, not leastly, to proudly decorate the field of battle. To delineate the lineage between friend and foe, heraldic symbols in rich colors were embroidered with silken threads into the garments of both men and women.

Shown here, a fanciful reproduction of a Medieval wedding.

Photographs courtesy of Rose D'Zynes. Photography by Seaton Ashley Galleries.

patterned lace appeared about the mid-sixteenth century and were, most likely, an out-growth of embroidery techniques.

Ladies' gowns were of rich fabrics, such as brocades, velvets, satin damasks, and pearl-sewn cloths of gold, thus explaining why the Renaissance was often referred to as "the Pearl Age." The East brought gems and tissue cloths of gold and silver, the North provided the luxurious elegance of furs. The bodice of the gown was generally snug and short-waisted, requiring corsets of heavy linen. The petticoat was of green or crimson satin. Early sleeves were long and tight, but later slashed and puffed to reveal the sheer undergarment. In Italy, the dress was soft, elegant, and fluid, a reflection of the idealization of the human form as noted in Italian Renaissance art. They were artistically designed and of rich fabrics, again featuring pearl-sewn, golden cloth, which was also reflected in bridal attire. Cloaks were adorned with glittering brooches, cords, and tassels. When worn, a jeweled

The bride in this 1993 Renaissance wedding was Diane Barr (nee Rose), founder of *Rose D'Zynes*; the groom is Michael Barr. With its overtones of the chosen period, the Excalibur Hotel in Las Vegas was deemed to be the perfect setting for this re-creation, with the ceremony taking place in their Canterbury Chapel. Invitations were designed as an illuminated page from the Book of Kells and sent in mailing tubes covered with a replica of a fifteenth century map. In a massive undertaking of skill and ingenuity, each of the 35 invited guests were measured and outfitted with Elizabethan and Italian Rennaissance costumes in preparation for the special day.

The bride's gown, in the mode of the Italian Rennaissance, was white with a gold forepart and a Spanish *surcote* of white *jacquard*. The Italian-style headdress was created from a 1940s lace bridal cap. She carried a gold grapevine wreath with white roses nestled in golden ivy. The Lady of Honor wore an Italian gown of teal brocade and velvet, which featured a coat with hanging sleeves. Her bouquet

belt or girdle often held small pouches where one could place *necessairies* like beaded rosaries and even feathered fans.

The hair was pulled back off the forehead, with a middle part and chignon. Earlier, the hair was formed into a ribbon-wound braid. Sometimes the front hair was cut short to just below the cheek and curled. A thin gauze or voile veil appeared to float back from the head. Juliet style caps were also popular. False hair (especially blonde) was often worn, as well as wigs fashioned of white and yellow silk. To complete this "fashion portrait," a single jewel, suspended from a chain, often graced the middle of the forehead. Usually parted in the middle and often crowned with a floral wreath, the bride's long flowing locks were of great significance, since they served to indicate virginity. At her coronation, even Catherine of Aragon, regal in white satin, left her hair hanging loose to signify the same.

was of white roses with one red rosebud and two white doves on a gilded birdcage. The ladies-in-waiting carried gold fans, each with a white rose. In contrast, the wreaths of the six bridal maidens were of gold with red and white roses.

The groom's Henry VIII stature seemed "made-to-order" for a Tudor-style gold doublet covered with a red-skirted jerkin and a fur-collared navy blue *shaube*, regally accented with a four foot, hand-crafted sword. The "best man" (a female!) sported the tunic-style of Charles the Bold and carried a staff with red roses decorating its orb. The groom and groomsmen wore ribbon rosettes centered with a red rose, and family members carried white feather fans adorned with a single red rose.

The wedding party and guests were led to the Excalibur's Canterbury Chapel by the sounds of a fifteenth century sham or oboe played by a single musician. Following the ceremony, the same musician escorted them to dinner and a performance of "King Arthur's Tournament." A private reception followed, featuring a wedding cake decorated with white crystals, a gold heart, and a pair of hand-painted white swans.

Men's hair varied from moderately short to shoulder length, often with ringlets or a fringe over the forehead. A toque or the beret-crowned hat with plume or jewel decorations covered the head. Originating in Italy, the beret was at first simply a piece of circular fabric, drawn together to fit the head by a string or band (the small bow seen today on the inside leather band encircling a man's hat is a survivor of that original string concept).

Weddings during the Renaissance were replete with customs reflective of the period. Escorting the bride to the church were a pair of young boys, each with rosemary tied around their sleeves. The groom's profession was also noted in the processional to the church. For instance, if he was a tailor, pieces of cloth were scattered along the route, if a carpenter, wood shavings fell in the path. The bride frequently carried, or was preceded by, a silver cup that held a branch of rosemary. The chief maidens (today's bridesmaids) carried golden garlands of wheat and bride cakes, both signifying fertility. The ceremony itself was apt to be a rowdy affair, with young men trying to snatch the garters of the groom and the laces of the bride even while the "solemn ceremony" was underway. The festivities to follow often lasted for days, and included dancing around what were then called bride bushes or bride stakes, a custom reminiscent of the "Maypole dance."

In Holland, the costumes of the time were generally austere, with black predominating. The French aristocracy, on the other hand, favored various shades of green and colors with fanciful names like "kiss-me-my-love," "wasted time," or "mortal sin." Rich textiles of velvet and satin in deep hues fell in natural folds and were decorated with wide lace and slim braids of gold. Men's costumes exhibited panache, being yet another indication of the volatile temperament and fierce sense of honor that dominated the period. It was, indeed, a time when "hearts were bold and men were men."

One of the mothers in a Rennaissance ceremony was resplendent in this burgundy gown with flowing train.

Shown here is a bridal gown indicative of the Cavalier period (1630-1650). Note the double layers, the underskirt delicately embroidered, the overskirt of quilted damask. The fanciful, pearl-enhanced ruff encircles the bride's head like a halo, and the full, decorative sleeves are gathered above the elbow.

Photograph courtesy of Rose D'Zynes

The "Marie Antoinette" look of the eighteenth century. This period saw the overskirt of the *polonaise* looped up along the sides, falling in festoons over the underskirt. Satin in straw-colors, yellows, pinks, and pale greens was popular, and *echelles*, ribbons that ran "ladder-like" down the center, were a popular decorative accent. Hair again reared its sometimes pretty, but more often outrageous, head, frequently rising a towering three feet!
Photograph courtesy of Rose D'Zynes

A modern wedding in the spirit of the French Empire period. The gown is a reproduction of a museum pattern from 1805. The garb of the groom and his attendant were inspired by the style that has traditionally been worn by those to be presented to the Royal Court (whether enlisted or civilian), resulting in the fanciful "Royal Prince" look.

Photograph courtesy of Rose D'Zynes

An eclectic Frontier wedding, combining a variety of 1845 attire.

Photograph courtesy of Rose D'Zynes

In a Frontier wedding ceremony performed at Lake Arrowhead in 1995, the gentlemen wore silk vests, black cutaways, hickory striped pants, and black gamblers' hats. The children's attire is equally authentic, the boy a miniature of his older counterparts, the girl with frilly dress and Western boots.

Photographs courtesy of Rose D'Zynes. Photography by Seatyn Ashley Galleries

Like figures from *Gone With the Wind,* the gentlemen in this Antebellum wedding wear ivory frock coats, tapestry vests, and plantation hats.

Photograph courtesy Rose D'Zynes. Photography by Rituals Photographic Arts

A circa 1853 Antebellum wedding of the Old South. Unlike previous times, during this historical period, the steel-wire hoop weighed only one half pound and caused little discomfort, thus enabling skirts to become wider and wider.

Photographs courtesy of Rose D'Zynes. Photography by Bonnie's Photography Studio

Union and Confederate—a modern-day wedding with a Civil War theme that embraced both sides of the Mason-Dixon line.

Photograph courtesy of Rose D'Zynes

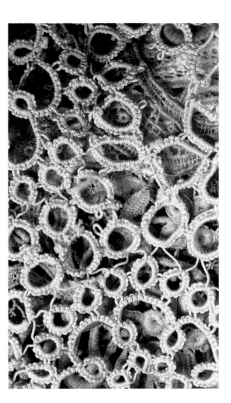

Victorian splendor—This bridal gown, with its bustle and long train, required yards and yards of fabric. Elegant ruffled edgings and a diaphanous veil, gathered at the back of the upswept hairdo, complete a most romantic picture.

Photograph courtesy of Rose D'Zynes

Fine examples of Victorian lacework and tatting, appropriate for a wedding shawl and to embellish the bridal gown.

Courtesy Jeannie Roberts

Bustle gown of 1874. Around 1875 the bustle *per se* took a short hiatus; however, all was not easily relinquished, for some modified padding was still carefully placed under petticoats. Long trains, tight at the ankles, became popular, adding to the illusion of slender height. The bustle returned again in the early years of the 1880s, growing in size during the second half of the decade. By 1885, materials became bulky and ponderously heavy.

Photograph courtesy of Rose D'Zynes. Photography by Bonnie's Photography Studio

Indicative of a later period of the Western frontier, this 1883 bustle gown features paisley brocade, a pearl-trimmed Chantilly lace overlay, silk sleeves with Venice lace, and handmade roses. Note the bouquet of roses mixed with wild flowers.

Photograph courtesy of Rose D'Zynes. Photograpy by Rituals Photographic Arts

The Victorian wedding party of 1894, interpreted for the modern bride who prefers to emulate the romance of the past. The setting was the Mission Inn in Riverside, California. Also shown is a close-up of the bride's magnificent Victorian cape. Although the veil was becoming less fashionable, many brides of the period still chose to wear them in more traditional fashion, but in a somewhat unusual way. Often the tulle was bunched at the top of the head by a hairdresser, and then allowed to fall to the edge of the skirt. It was split in the center to above the forehead and a fine cord was threaded through the fabric above the front of the hair, enabling the maid of honor to simply slide it, like a curtain, to each side at the proper time. In this Victorian re-creation *(left)*, the groomsmen sport a British "Ascot" look, replete with grey cutaways, grey trousers, spats, vests, striped ties, bell toppers, gloves, and canes.

Photographs courtesy of Rose D'Zynes.
Photography by Rituals Photographic Arts

A bridal attendant and groomsman in Gay Nineties attire reflect the more playful attitude of the times.
Photograph courtesy of Rose D'Zynes. Photography by Rituals Photographic Arts

Wedding participants of the 1894 Western frontier. Although with the solemn look of an old tintype, female styles had become more daring and provocative. Note the open-lace black gloves.

Photograph courtesy of Rose D'Zynes

Museum reproductions of Edwardian style 1914 garb. The gentleman wears a *pebble la toi* cutaway, derby hat, and ascot tie. The lady personifies the elegance of the period. Even though King Edward died in 1910, the English Edwardian period was generally considered as the time between the turn-of-the-century and World War I.

Photograph courtesy of Rose D'Zynes

An Edwardian bridal couple. She is radiant in a silky "pigeon-breasted" gown with full sleeves and lace trim. Her hair is rolled back in the style of the day. The groom wears formal *pebble la toi* tail coat, black vest, wing tip collar, and black bow tie. A top hat completed the outfit.

Courtesy of Rose D'Zynes. Photograph by Rituals Photograpic Arts

The bride of 1923.

King Constantine of Greece and his bride Anne Marie, following their 1964 wedding.

HISTORICAL AND SOCIALLY PROMINENT UNIONS

"I chose my wife, as she did her wedding gown, for qualities that would wear well."

Goldsmith

Social standing among the elite reached its apex in America and Europe during the Victorian period. Status was all, and young ladies who were of the highest echelon and married well became a form of royalty to the masses, their comings and goings, marriages and intrigues, enabling ordinary citizens to live vicariously through them. Not content with mere gossip, the most finite detail was devoured by an eager public. For instance, as reported in a March 6, 1897 British newspaper account, titled "Fashionable Marriage" regarding the union of Mr. Vivian H. Smith and Lady Sybil Mary McDonnell:

> "The bride's dress was of plain white moire velous, with full court train elegantly trimmed with fine old family Brussels lace. She wore a long Brussels lace veil over orange-blossoms, and she carried a bridal bouquet of rare white exotics."

Not to be outdone in the celebrity idolatry department, the American public was as fascinated then as they are now with weddings involving royalty and the socially connected . . . and most especially so when that union joined the royal personage with an American heiress, as was the case in 1907 when Gloria Vanderbilt married Hungarian Count Szechenyi (who was impeccably attired in full military regalia, including medals, swords, and furs). As might be expected in this socially-driven era, the Vanderbilts were not alone in the "race toward royalty" sweepstakes, for entrepreneur Jay Gould's daughter Anna chose a French count.

The wedding of Fay Goelet to the Duke of Roxburghe in 1904 created a particular stir among the populace, an interest that wasn't lost on the media. As described in the New York Press:

> "The wedding was simplicity itself, but the scene without and within the church where the wedding took place was one of the most amazing ever witnessed in the city of New York. Thousands of women, impelled by curiosity and forgetful of gentleness or of ordinary delicacy, pushed, hauled, surged, and

The late-fourteenth-century second marriage of St. Etheldreda (St. Andry) to the King of Northumbria

95

The marriage of Ferdnand de Medici, Duke of Tuscany, and Christine of Lorraine. She wears an enormous collar of *godrannée* lace.

Aurore Dupin, who later became known as George Sand, confronted the iron will of a domineering mother, who left no stone unturned in an effort to force her daughter into marriage. The equally stubborn and fiercely independent Aurore resorted to a hunger strike, becoming so ill that her mother relented and sent her to the home of one of her father's army friends for a visit. Fasting was not without its rewards, for it was there that she met her future husband. Apparently the marriage wasn't "made in heaven," for some time later, another visit again bore results . . . at the home of Franz Liszt's mistress, Sand met Frederic Chopin, with whom she had a torrid love affair!

Richard Burton, the nineteenth century British explorer, would seem an unlikely candidate for falling under the spell of "love at first sight." However, as he strolled down a boulevard in Boulogne, France, he turned to stare at two pretty girls, Isabel Arundell and her sister. "Isabel trembled under his gaze. 'That man will marry me,' she told her sister. The next day he returned with a piece of chalk and wrote on the wall: 'May I speak to you?' Isabel picked up the chalk and replied: "No, mother will be angry.'"[2] Although they met only briefly in the interim, it wasn't until four years later that love blossomed, and a full ten years after they first met that Richard Burton and Isabel Arundell finally married.

"It is said Queen Victoria 'put the question' to Prince Albert by showing him Windsor and its beauties and the distant landscape, and then quietly saying, 'All this may be yours.'"

Good Form and Social Ethics, *Fannie Dickerson Chase*, 1913, as reported in *Wedded Bliss*

fought to get into the church; to get close to the carriage of the frightened bride; to carry off souvenirs; to touch the bridal robes; and to do a hundred and one other things, creating such an uproar and confusion that a platoon of police, armed with nightsticks, was actually compelled to charge upon them and, in many instances, to use force. . . . They fought, scratched, and screeched like a parcel of wildcats disputing a quarry."[3]

Several decades later, one of the most notable and highly-publicized unions of the twentieth century—and followed with intense interest around the world—took place. In this instance, however, the circumstances of the King's abdication for "the woman I love" stripped the Duke of Windsor's wedding to Wallis Warfield Simpson of the ceremonial splendor normally decreed for royalty. The future Duchess "wore a floor-length cocktail dress with a fitted jacket, wrist length gloves, high-heeled sandals, and a tiny skull-type hat, all colored 'Wallis blue.' The same hue prevailed in her trousseau of 80 dresses and 40 hats. The Duke wore formal black morning clothes."[4]

> 🔖 *"In 1909 someone calculated that more than 500 American heiresses had married titled foreigners who had thus raked in a total of about $220,000,000."*[5]
>
> 🔖 *"Leonard Jerome, lawyer, whose sole previous claim to prominence had been his marriage to 'the most beautiful girl in Palmyra, N.Y.,' blew $10,000 on a Delmonico's debut for his daughter Jennie—an investment that paid off when she married Lord Randolph Churchill (and later became the mother of Sir Winston)."*[6]
>
> 🔖 *All was not happy for American heiress Consuelo Vanderbilt. Fearful that her tearful daughter would choose to disappear rather than marry mummy's choice, the socially-acceptable Duke of Marlborough, her mother stationed guards outside Consuelo's bedroom to prevent her possible escape—and the ensuing social disgrace.*

The acerbic wit of Charles Dana Gibson.

A decorative impression of the wedding of Miss Gloria Morgan to Mr. Reginald C. Vanderbilt.

The bride, her matron of honor, Mrs. Glenn Stewart, and Constance, Countess de Maupas, sister of the bride.

The Morgans and the Vanderbilts unite, as depicted in the April 1923 issue of *Harper's Bazar*.

Circa 1929, the wedding portrait of Mrs. John Davis Lodge, nee Francesca Braggiotti. John Lodge, who also had an acting and movie career, later became Governor of Connecticut.

The royal gathering at the marriage of King Alexander I of Yugoslovia to Princess Marie of Romania. The groom is second from the left, his bride to his left, and Queen Marie occupying the central position.

Bedecked in medals, King Zog of Albania with his bride Queen Geraldine, following their 1938 wedding.

"Princess Anne of France—the only royal bride this year—wore this lovely wedding gown of crepe satin made on simple lines. It is by Worth." The gown is further described as having "... a surplice bodice and a graceful pointed drapery at the side of the skirt held by sprays of orange blossoms and a long court-train hanging straight from the shoulders with a veil of priceless lace ..."
"The Summer Bride,"
Delineator, *June, 1928*

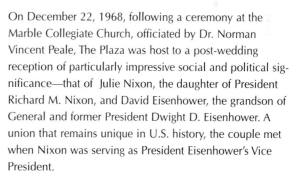

New York City's Plaza Hotel has been the site of many prestigious wedding receptions. In 1910 this magnificent edifice towered over the landscape of Central Park (above); by 1930 that same landscape had already become home to an ever-growing influx of skyscrapers (left).

On December 22, 1968, following a ceremony at the Marble Collegiate Church, officiated by Dr. Norman Vincent Peale, The Plaza was host to a post-wedding reception of particularly impressive social and political significance—that of Julie Nixon, the daughter of President Richard M. Nixon, and David Eisenhower, the grandson of General and former President Dwight D. Eisenhower. A union that remains unique in U.S. history, the couple met when Nixon was serving as President Eisenhower's Vice President.

Photographs courtesy of The Plaza Hotel

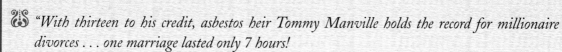

"With thirteen to his credit, asbestos heir Tommy Manville holds the record for millionaire divorces ... one marriage lasted only 7 hours!

When searching for a second wife, and enamored of Mina Miller, Thomas Edison wrote in his diary, "Saw a lady who looked like Mina. Got to thinking about Mina and came near being run over by a streetcar. If Mina interferes much more will have to take out an accident policy."[7]

The inimitable Greta Garbo and her dashing leading man, Robert Taylor, in a scene from *Camille,* the classic 1936 film adapted from Alexander Dumas' tale of tragedy and sacrifice.

Photograph courtesy of the Joan Castle Joseff archives

BRIDES AND COURTING ON THE SILVER SCREEN

The "movies" not only revolutionized the entertainment industry but captured the heart of America and the world in very personal and profound ways. Even in its infancy, this new-fangled invention exerted an enormous and unexpected power, influencing social and political issues far beyond what most pundits would have predicted or even deemed possible.

Like the blossom being plucked by Tyrone Power (pictured with co-star Wanda Hendrix), romance bloomed in medieval Italy in *The Prince of Foxes*, a 1949 costume epic.

Photograph courtesy of the Joan Castle Joseff archives

Whether in silent flicks or "talkies," black and white or technicolor, the silver screen

touched a chord in the American psyche. Audiences sat transfixed as they experienced a gamut of emotions—tears at the anguish of war, laughter at the escapism of sophisticated, high-society comedies. In big cities and small towns, the public clamored for more, often standing patiently in line for hours to garner the "magic seat" that ensured them a few hours of delicious escapism.

The public hungered for tales of love in good times and bad, and Hollywood did not disappoint! Week after week, year after year, movie moguls released a barrage of films, some steeped in pure fantasy, others replete with the trials and tribulations of lives that resonated with familiarity within one's own peer group. There were sagas of kings and emperors, bad guys and good guys, intrigue and mystery, old-fashioned courtships, heart-stopping romances (will the star-crossed lovers ever be united?)—and, of course—brides, brides, brides!

Perhaps the most famous fictional lovers of all time—here is the wedding scene from Irving Thalberg's 1936 production of *Romeo and Juliet,* starring Leslie Howard as Romeo and Thalberg's wife Norma Shearer as Juliet.

Photograph courtesy of the Joan Castle Joseff archives

Happy ending—Richard Greene and Barbara Hale become "man and wife" in the 1951 film *Lorna Doone.*
Photograph courtesy of the Joan Castle Joseff archives

A lovers' triangle—Armando Silvestre shows Ricardo Montalban the engagement ring he's just given Cyd Charisse in 1951's *The Mark of the Renegade.* (The plot will undoubtedly "thicken," for the dashing Montalban looks just a wee bit jealous!)
Photograph courtesy of the Joan Castle Joseff archives

The screen's most famous "lover" and early matinee idol, Rudolph Valentino (whose appeal wasn't diminished by the "silent film" genre), is portrayed here by Tony Dexter (with Donna Drake) in the 1951 biographical film *Valentino.*

Photograph courtesy of the Joan Castle Joseff archives

From their tenth film together (*The Barclay's of Broadway, circa 1949*), Ginger Rogers and Fred Astaire, the most famous dancing partners of all time—she looking just as beautiful and he as debonaire as when they first performed together in 1933's *Flying Down to Rio*.
Photograph courtesy of the Joan Castle Joseff archives

Loretta Young and Warner Baxter pose in a film still from *Wife, Husband and Friend*—1939's screen version of "happily ever after"!

Photograph courtesy of the Joan Castle Joseff archives

Ann Sothern and Barry Sullivan are enraptured by each other—and the moonlight—in *Nancy Goes to Rio,* a 1950 Technicolor musical.

Photograph courtesy of the Joan Castle Joseff archives

Olivia de Havilland—not looking the happy bride—in a film still from *My Cousin Rachel,* circa 1952.

Photograph courtesy of the Joan Castle Joseff archives

It's never too late for romance to blossom, as the "matrimonially inclined" Spring Byington (shown here with Charles Coburn) is torn between two suitors in *Louisa,* a 1950 film that also starred Ronald Reagan.

Photograph courtesy of the Joan Castle Joseff archives

Perfection—Shown here in a scene from Walter Wanger's *Vogues of 1938,* the beauteous screen star Joan Bennett typifies the elegant formality of the 1930s bride.
Cinema Arts *magazine, July 1937*

*I*N LOVE AND WAR . . .
ROMANCE IN THE MILITARY

There's something about a man in uniform . . .

Throwing caution to the wind, romance catches fire during the tribulations of wartime. Fear for one's beloved and the pain of separation—often lengthy but temporary, sometimes tragically permanent—served to compound the deepest of bittersweet emotions.

This depiction of a Civil War wedding *(opposite page)* is titled "Till Death Us Do Part." As described, "The ages-old wedding ceremony is an affirmation of life in the dark times of war. Garlands of flowers and the marital trappings of the young Southern Confederacy combine as symbols of love, honor, and hope. It is a joyous occasion clouded by an uncertain future."

Courtesy of D.J. Neary, Artist

A group of World War I doughboys take time to pose for a photo.

War or peace, the attraction is ageless . . . for the mere image of a man in uniform weaves a special brand of magic. From the Roman gladiators and noble knights (with armor to match the shine in fair damsel's eyes) to Yankee doughboys in World War I and RAF airmen in World War II, that man in uniform, be he ancient or modern, was destined to cast a hypnotic spell on those he left behind.

Proudly displaying a heavy burden of Austrian military medals, the emperor enchants Joan Fontaine in 1948's *The Emperor Waltz*.

Photograph courtesy of the Joan Castle Joseff archives

U.S. "doughboy" *(left)* in 1919; U.S. serviceman in 1947 *(right)*.

History and literature are replete with tales (either factual or embellished fiction) of wartime heartbreak and sad farewells. Recent times haven't altered this mystique, for even today a stiff-backed West Point or Naval Academy cadet in impeccably tailored uniform—at ease or passing in review—cannot fail to impress, and cause many a feminine heart to flutter!

It is well documented through descriptions, paintings, photographs, and even motion pictures, that innumerable personages of royalty and high rank have arrayed themselves in full military regalia for the wedding day. Complete with formal uniforms, swords, medals, and epaulets, such garb befits the pomp and pageantry that was expected, while at the same time surrounding its wearer with an aura of splendor—and power.

Although she co-starred with the dashing John Hodiak, Ann Southern can't disguise her attraction to a U.S. Marine in this scene from the 1944 film *Maisie Goes to Reno*.
Photograph courtesy of the Joan Castle Joseff archives

Frances Gifford and James Craig seem to have eyes only for each other in this scene from 1947's *Army Brat*. (Her beauty and his uniform surely added impetus to the romance!)
Photograph courtesy of the Joan Castle Joseff archives

"Graduation" by Thomas Webb (1885-1975).
Photograph courtesy Alan M. Goffman, American Illustration

Let's Dance! These dance cards are from the West Point Military Academy, circa 1927.

Military Regulation uniforms are the required wedding attire to be worn by all men in the service, in accordance with official orders, for the duration. This applies not only to the men in the Army, but also to those in the other branches of the armed forces as well—the Navy and the Marines.

Pertinent, considering the servicemen married during World War II, a 1940s "Guide to Good Grooming" article in Esquire *succinctly included the military when discussing proper male wedding attire:*
"Military: Regulation uniforms are the required wedding attire to be worn by all men in the service, in accordance with official orders, for the duration."

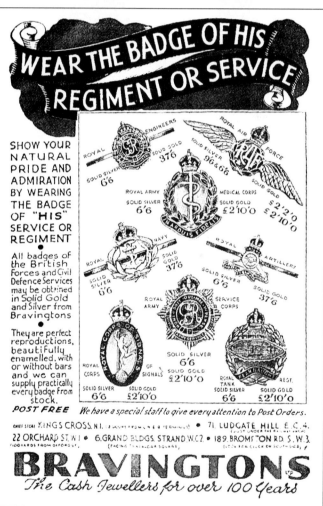

This ad appeared in a 1940 British military booklet (note that it was geared to mothers, wives, and sweethearts of British servicemen—"Show your natural pride and admiration by wearing the badge of 'his' service or regiment.") For the purpose of comparing pound sterling values then (approximately $5 U.S.) to those of an American army private, it would have cost about $10 to obtain the solid gold Royal Tank Corps badge, or nearly half a month's pay.

Courtesy Charles Edwards

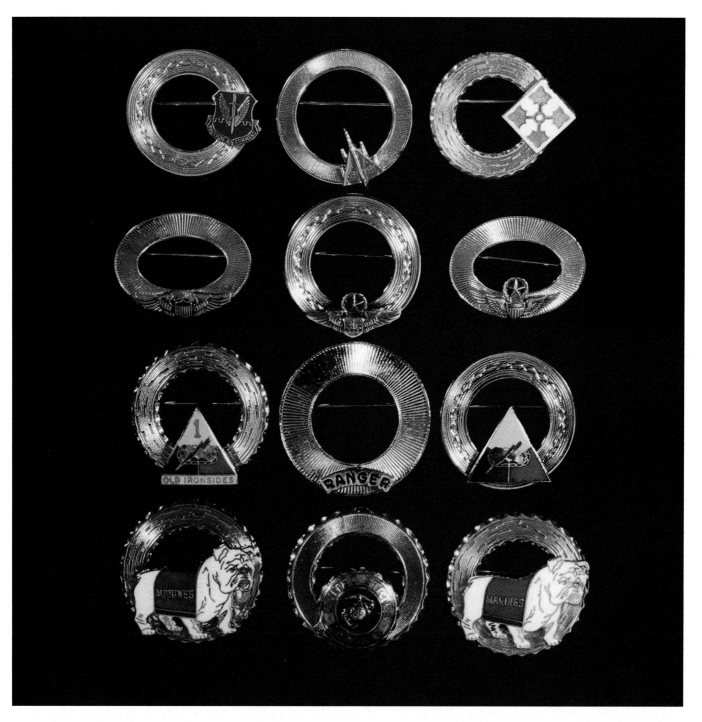

A love token from servicemen and those in military academies, these sweetheart pins are a cross-section from various branches of the service, and were often worn as mementos (and a sign of commitment) by "the girls they left behind."

A symbol of support, patriotism, and love, sweetheart pins—or badge brooches—were worn most specifically during the twentieth century, and served as treasured gifts from servicemen to their wives and sweethearts. Still collected and proudly worn, the styles are seemingly endless—some simple, others elaborately enameled and jeweled, with many of precious metals and with the quality of fine jewelry. An unusual fashion accessory of today, they nevertheless continue to serve as an ongoing reminder of sacrifice and commitment.

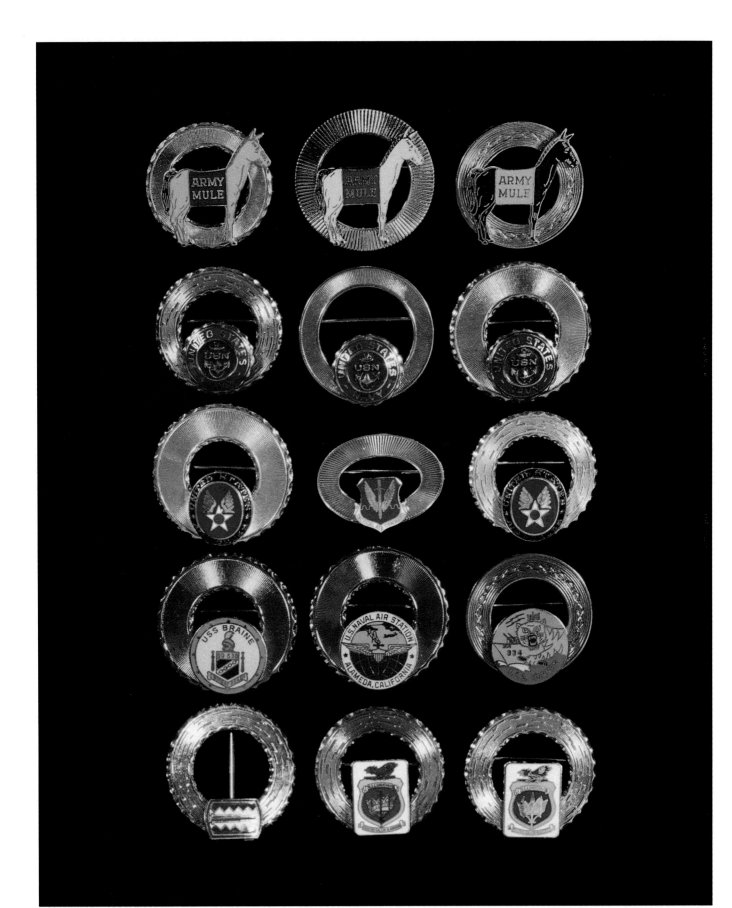

"You're in Our Hearts" by Howard Chandler Christie, and reproduced as a World War II poster.

Photograph courtesy Alan M. Goffman, American Illustrations

After the War! By Pat Holbrooke/Thomas Webb, this tempera on board illustration is titled "Couple Kissing," and appeared in the August 25, 1945 issue of *Liberty Magazine*.

Photograph courtesy Alan M. Goffman, American Illustration

After the wedding—"House Plans" by artist Gene Pelham.

"Our New Silverware" by Coles Phillips (1880-1927); gouache on artist board.

Photograph courtesy Alan M. Goffman, American Illustration

*H*APPILY EVER AFTER

"Farewell to the bride! May her path through life be ever strewn with thornless roses."

Herman Patrick Tappe *(Harper's Bazar)*, May 1922

The ceremony is over. The festivities that follow are not only a celebration of the marriage, but also an opportunity to wish the newlyweds well as they embark on their marital journey. Requiring careful planning, the reception brings family and friends together in what will most likely be the most important celebration of the couple's life.

From travel arrangements to suitcases filled with appropriate attire, the honeymoon that follows demands yet more pre-planning. The couple's return also requires considerable forethought. From furniture, china, and silver to linens and home accessories, it's yet another important task in the wedding scenario.

Far right: "Nothing ever takes the place of silver" . . . a 1926 advertisement to capture the attention of the bride-to-be.

Below: Gorham Silverware advertisement, circa 1919.

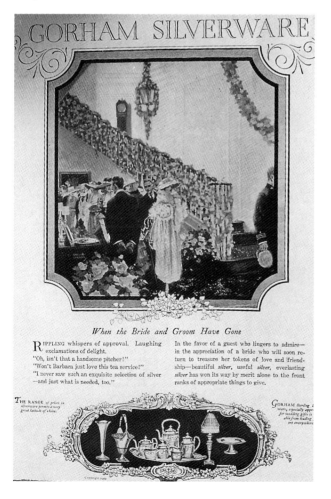

In preparation for married life (from the mundane "necessities lists" to the elegant linens and tableware) some suggestions and tips from the Marshall Field & Co. *Bride's Book,* circa 1937.

Newly wedded bliss highlighted by charming china figurines.

Complete with cupids and flowers tucked into the napkins, a wedding reception at The City Midday Club in lower Manhattan.

Photograph courtesy Atlas Floral Decorators, Inc.

Charming jewelry in memory of the reception . . . brooches and earrings of champagne glasses, champagne bucket with bottle (and corkscrew earrings to open it with), and even a bowl of caviar with golden spoon.

Courtesy A Piece of the Rainbow

Covered with rose-colored, hand-set stones both front and back, puffed-heart minaudeures. The larger could be used by the bride at the reception; the smaller one would make a charming accent for the attendants to carry during the ceremony (and serve as a gift for them, as well).

Courtesy A Piece of the Rainbow

May I have this dance? The bride and groom and an attendant couple take to the floor in two charming brooches (the rhinestone skirts hang free, giving movement to the piece).

Courtesy A Piece of the Rainbow

Ready for the trousseau—wide-leg panties and matching bra, circa 1930s are overshadowed by a boudoir bag *(above)*. Coordinating with the undergarments, the close-up is of a lace appliqued *peignoir* decorated with a romantically-inspired vintage porcelain pin *(right)*.

Lingerie courtesy Dorothy Louise Gillette; boudoir bag courtesy Catherine Stein; pin courtesy Alyson French.

THE TROUSSEAU

Choosing a trousseau is often nearly equal in importance to the bride's wedding day apparel. This has been true for decades, although many wedding trips in earlier times were of far longer duration than those of today, requiring more careful attention to wardrobe. Extensive travel, involving weeks and even months, naturally put a great strain on the new bride. An attractive persona was understandably important, while her wardrobe needed to accommodate any eventuality. It was a challenging task involving minute planning . . . and a host of trunks!

Showing off the wedding finery—this oil on canvas by renowned illustrator McClelland Barclay (1891-1943), who lost his life in the Pacific in World War II, was reproduced as an advertisement for Lux Soap in 1927.

Photograph courtesy Alan M. Goffman, American Illustration.

The April 1923 issue of *Vogue* elaborates on this in some detail when describing the trousseau of a French bride:

"In France, any young girl who is about to be married . . . will doubtless talk of the pleasure . . . in packing her trunk for the wedding journey. . . . Usually the journey lasts no longer than three weeks or a month; therefore, in packing one should combine a large amount of chic in a small amount of space." The article then goes on to recommend: "one dozen chemise, three or four combinations for day wear, two . . . for evening . . . six nightgowns, and as many brassieres and step ins for those who have not accustomed themselves to the mode of 'less underneath'—that is to say, the sans culottes." Also suggested were cotton stockings, silk stockings, girdles and pyjamas. "The slippers or mules have acquired today an elegance which equals that of evening slippers; one may have them to match each pair of pyjamas or each peignoir, and this fad is so popular that it is not necessary to go to the biggest shoe shops to buy these frivolities of soft green or red leather edged with swan's-down and maribou. The mule, which can be made in cloth of gold or silver is often outlined with uncurled ostrich tips . . ."

For milady's trousseau, a French-made silk purse with prong set paste gems and metallic needlework; circa early 1900s.

Courtesy Jeannie Roberts

The tradespeople upon whom the bride was dependent for her trousseau were an important, and not to be overlooked, contingent for, ". . . not all brides have a decorated church, full choir . . . and the like, but all brides have trousseaux. From the village maiden who runs tucks in simple muslin for months beforehand to the wearer of the $2,000 veil, every bride makes more or less preparation as to costume."

"Hail to the Easter Bride" by Kate Hopkins
The Designer, April 1913

Wedding trousseau items, as illustrated in a ca. 1920s magazine.

FOR THE CORNERS OF THE TROUSSEAU

Assembling a trousseau— with help from the Marshall Field & Co. *Bride's Book*, circa 1937.

It's the accessorizing amenities (and what's underneath) that count . . . for the wedding day and the bride's trousseau, a 1920 advertisement for silk hosiery and another from 1926 for "intimate apparel."

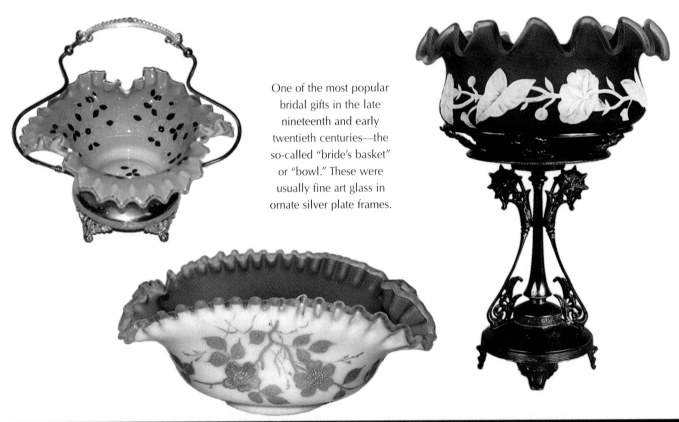

One of the most popular bridal gifts in the late nineteenth and early twentieth centuries—the so-called "bride's basket" or "bowl." These were usually fine art glass in ornate silver plate frames.

Crown Milano bowl on stand, about 1893-1900. New Bedford, Massachusetts, Mt. Washington Glass Works; opaque white glass, mold-blown, enameled and gilded; stand of quadruple plate by Pairpoint Manufacturing Company.
Photograph courtesy the Corning Museum of Glass

GIFTS AND MEMENTOS

Whether to the bride of social prominence and wealth or the peasant of Medieval times, gifts have always been proferred to the newlyweds. There is also a tradition of gift-giving between brides and grooms and from each of them to their attendants. In large weddings, and those of the socially prominent, the gifts were usually displayed for guests to view (although it was considered bad taste to show the accompanying cards, thus deterring the inevitable "comparisons"). Such displays were especially important during Victorian times, and it was a tradition that continued well into the twentieth century.

Treasured silver pieces—two groupings
of Victorian silver spoons and servers.
Courtesy Barbra Music Designs

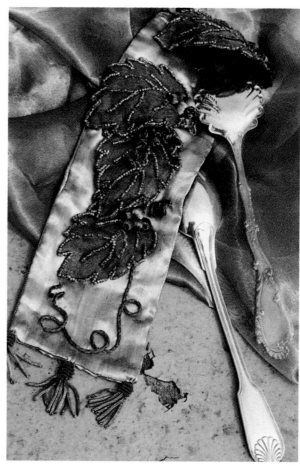

One particularly popular gift had its beginnings during the Victorian period. It was the "bride's basket"; however, then they weren't baskets at all but bowls nestled in silverplated holders. Running the gamut from towering edifices, resembling epigernes, to simple basket styles, what are generally referred to among collectors today as "brides' baskets" didn't actually garner that name until much later in the twentieth century. Although the term was used as early as 1919, even then it didn't signify fruit and berry bowls with metal holders, but instead, silver baskets shaped like handled vases.

Reflecting the eclectic tastes of the Victorians, the vintage styles designated as brides' baskets today were influenced by a host of historical periods—from Rococo to Greek and Roman and into the newly discovered beauties of Art Nouveau. Overall, the category encompasses a plethora of styles finished in various types of metal. The glass bowls were designed to accommodate not only "goodies" like fruits and sweets, but also flowers, and some were dually impressive when fashioned as candelabrum. Encompassing a wide range of styles and materials, they were produced by prestigious glass houses in the United States and abroad that were famous for glass types such as Crown Milano, cameo, and New England peach blow and Burmese. Some were enameled with flowers and leaves, even fruit and birds, others were of American patterned glass, like the popular hobnail and coin-dot patterns.

"For the most part, the bowls of the Brides' Baskets are in the shape of shells, many with quite deeply crimped and fluted edges, somehow reminiscent of a colorful petticoat assailed by a stiff breeze."[1] Nonetheless, there were a seemingly endless variety of shapes and applications. Glass was sometimes ribbed and cut, with the bowls ranging in size from four or five inches to a foot or more in diameter. Colors were as vast as the tastes of the purchasers, ranging from pastels to deep reds to the somewhat gaudier "carnival glass" colorations.

Times, of course, do change . . . and prices with them, for these lovely remembrances from yesterday could be purchased for as little as $1.50 in 1905!

The ultimate in fine giftware for late Victorian brides—fine American cut glass from the so-called Brilliant Period. From the 1880s to World War I, heavy, ornately cut glass, in pieces large and small, was cherished by all brides. Today collectors vie for the finest examples, which are both rare and expensive.

From bride to groom . . . an ornate cut glass humidor. Circa 1890-1900

105

So Jack is stepping off . . . . !

"To the bride of the happiest man on earth"—a gift! But what shall it be? What token of their friendship will mean all things to her—and so to him? What gift will voice their unspoken thoughts upon his wedding day?

Shall we tell them? Why not? It is Sterling! Sterling for its unquestioned beauty. Sterling for its true and lasting worth. Sterling because she wishes it more than all things else—evidence of lifelong friendship for him, and now for her.

STERLING SILVERSMITHS GUILD OF AMERICA

It is Sterling
~more can not be said

This 1926 advertisement encourages the groom to give his bride a gift of sterling silver.

> Suggested as gifts from groom to best man and ushers: "a gold clip for bank notes; a key chain with crystal medallion; cuff links of garnet, lapis and other precious stones; traveling pocket watch with luminous dial . . ."
>
> "For the Well Dressed Man—How to Dress Properly for the Formal and Informal Wedding,"
> Vanity Fair, May 1926
>
> "At Saks Fifth Avenue order match-books pristine and white, with your initials and those of your fiance stamped in silver, with the date of the wedding."
> Vogue, April 1939

A magnificent gift for the wedding couple (or for each to give the other) this lava cameo brooch in high relief, along with the matching cuff links, is set in gold and date from the 1800s.

Courtesy Jeannie Roberts

"Our idea of a dandy wedding gift is this handsome ticker cased in fine saddle leather. For the domicile, it stands proudly open to show its face and those of two near-and-dear ones. For travelling (starting with the honeymoon itself), it folds its tent like the Arabs and buckles up tightly, protectingly. $5 at Hammacher Schlemmer."

"Just Looking Thanks," *Mademoiselle,* June 1940

Typical of a wedding gift display in the Victorian/Edwardian tradition—*top left to bottom right:* heavily-decorated Capodimonte covered dish, replete with cupids and angels in high relief; heavily embossed giant urn; small cut glass-style compote with pedestal base; cast-iron lamp with small hanging bowl to hold oil and a floating wick.

From the mid-nineteenth century, charming "tussie mussies." These not only provided decorative accents on the wedding day, but also made lovely wedding gifts.

Courtesy Jeannie Roberts

An excess in gift giving was partially described in a March 6, 1897 British newspaper article reporting on the marriage of Mr. Vivian H. Smith and Lady Sybil Mary McDonnell:

". . . The presents—between four and five hundred—included from the Queen (the Countess being one of her Ladies-in-Waiting) a jewelled and enameled pendant, in a design of shamrock, rose, and thistle. The English flower is in pink enamel with a diamond and ruby centre, the Scotch in emerald and diamonds, and the Irish native shamrocks in enamel dew-dropped with diamonds. Prince Henry of Battenberg's present was a unique little ormalu and ebony clock with two carved ivory figures at the base."[2]

The "china of choice" for many brides of yesteryear and today, this dainty Lenox pitcher personifies the classic lines so representative of their enduring designs.

The ultimate for an elegant dinner party . . . these napkin holders, circa 1930s, are of lustrous metal, each centered with a colorful stone and an etched glass faceted flat handle.

Courtesy Jeannie Roberts

🕸 *Pearls of wisdom—In ancient Rome it was believed that marital happiness would be assured as long as the bride wore pearls. During the Crusades, pearls were the most popular choice as a knight's gift to his beloved on their wedding day.*

🕸 *Describing the pre-wedding and wedding festivities of her cousin Betty's marriage in Salem, Ohio, in 1900, Theodate Pope wrote in her diary, "We have done nothing but open the boxes and show off to callers the presents." And later, "After dinner we surrounded Betty in the living room while she undid the boxes that came today . . . one box was as big as a trunk with three enormous silver dishes in it."³*

🕸 *Desperate times and circumstances often called for desperate (but effective) measures. In villages in Great Britain, a simple cart was used for the journey to the wedding site. The longer the journey, the better the outcome . . . for stops were made at every dwelling along the way, in the hope that by the time they reached the church the cart would be filled with enough household items—even furniture—to start the couple on their lifelong matrimonial journey!*

From the March 1913 issue of the *Ladie's Home Journal,* needlework gifts for the bride.

A JOURNEY THROUGH PERIODICALS OF THE DAY

Gifts for the wedding party were expected to be chosen with care, as shown in this excerpt from the May 1923 issue of Harper's Bazar: *"From groom to bride, father to bride, or bridesmaid to bride, how beautiful the choices. Picture a gold locket inlaid with a border of black enamel with a deco-style Greek design in which she can place a treasured photo of her loved one or even a snippet of the bridal veil. More conventional, but always lovely and never out of style, a short string of nacreous pearls could last a lifetime . . . and even become a treasured heirloom. Or how about an exquisite vanity case, striped with gold and decorated with enamel, to compactly hold milady's essentials, like a fluffy powder puff, lipstick, and even the ever-necessary pad and pencil." The same issue also suggested canes, gold-tipped with a monogram for the ushers, cigarette cases, lozenge-shaped engraved cuff links in gold for the ushers, and watches, earrings and bracelets set with precious gems and carvings for the bride from her groom.*

From the bride to her attendants—sparkling photo frames of hand-set stones.

Courtesy A Piece of the Rainbow.

"Show us the woman who won't care for these lovelies and we'll show you a crab with no appreciation of beauty . . . reproductions in sterling silver, no less—of Georgian hurricane candlesticks, their clear crystal globes grape-etched. 11" high and for our money a real bargain at $7.50 a pair (or $3.75 each)."

"Just Looking Thanks," *Mademoiselle*, June 1940

A gift from the groom to his attendants—champagne bottle cuff links and matching key chain.
Courtesy A Piece of the Rainbow

From the 1940s, these feminine accessories made appropriate gifts from bride to attendants: with its bar closing and lipstick container, the Yardley compact is unique; the purse-size perfume container is of engraved sterling.

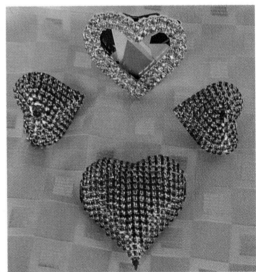

Attendants' gifts in remembrance of a romantic day. At top, heart-shaped frame, below heart brooch and matching earrings.
Courtesy A Piece of the Rainbow

For the bridal attendants . . . looking like gaily-wrapped gift boxes, brooches that open to reveal four miniature frames.
Courtesy A Piece of the Rainbow

A touch of romance for the honey-moon. Rose heart pin and matching earrings.

Courtesy A Piece of the Rainbow

Gold hearts brooches—each with open, basket weave setting and amethyst heart in center.

Courtesy A Piece of the Rainbow

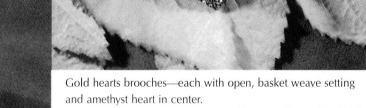

Click . . . click! Honeymoon memories in three-dimensional camera brooches of hand-set stones.

Courtesy A Piece of the Rainbow

From *The Delineator,* couture designs for brides of 1928 *(right and facing page.)*

Madeleine Vionnet's conception of the wedding gown is a sheath of lustrous white crepe satin, drawn tightly around the figure and forming a long train.

Vionnet

HERE COMES THE MILLENIUM . . . COUTURE AND FASHION BRIDES AT CENTURY'S END

From those first inhabitants in the Garden of Eden to modern-day icons, each coupling of two distinct personalities is destined to create a unique experience. In addition, the ever-changing predilections of both fashion and prevailing social mores have always influenced bridal attire. From stylish trendsetters of bygone days—be they in ancient Rome or the court of Marie Antoinette— to modern-day couturiers, all have left their imprint on not only daily and seasonal fashions but what is probably the most momentous selection of all . . . the gown chosen for the bride's walk down the aisle and those first tentative steps on her marital journey.

Molyneux

Worth

Lanvin

Louiseboulanger

Louiseboulanger's creation *(bottom left)* is of cream-colored lace with a graceful, dropping skirt, indicative of the period.

Princess Anne of France wore the Worth creation of crepe satin with flowing train.

The Lanvin frock of white taffeta was reminiscent of the Victorian era. The taffeta bodice has a yoke and cape of tulle, all complementary to the delicate tiers of ruffles on the skirt.

Captain Molyneux caused a sensation when he showed this bridal gown of pale yellow georgette, which trailed into a long train. Completing this colorful picture was a veil of pink tulle.

143

It is not happenstance that couture runway showings traditionally feature wedding gown finales or that many designers have created a specific niche by concentrating solely on wedding garb. Whether a Victorian style in 1900, a Molyneux creation in 1920, or a Priscilla of Boston confection from the 1990s, the 20th century has provided a plethora of designs, all fashioned to complement the ever radiant bride.

Far more appealing than two of life's undeniable certainties, death and taxes, is a third . . . the universal appeal of romance and weddings. It is thus inevitable that as the upcoming millennium unfolds, evolving societal changes and innovative couturiers will wield yet more influence on this most magical of days.

From designer Betsey Johnson's Spring 1996 fashion show . . . a bridal gown that any young lady would covet.
Photograph courtesy Betsey Johnson; photo by Dan Lecca

Couturier splendor . . . this bridal confection by Vivienne Westwood.
Photograph courtesy Vivienne Westwood, London

The following pages feature a sampling of Spring and Fall 1996 gowns by the Priscilla of Boston bridal fashion house.

Courtesy of Priscilla of Boston; photography by Hornick/Rivlin Studio

From the 1960s, an "A line" gown by Priscilla of Boston of silk cloud peau de soie with pearl accents at hem, sleeves, and crowning the veil.

Priscilla of Boston

Priscilla of Boston was founded 50 years ago by Priscilla Kidder. Her vision was to offer individually constructed gowns of the finest fabrics and laces, all under the aegis of fine designers and skilled artisans. Renowned for quality and design, Priscilla of Boston gowns have been chosen for many auspicious weddings. Among countless others, presidential daughters Lucy Johnson, and Julie and Tricia Nixon wore bridal gowns by Priscilla of Boston, and Princess Grace (nee Grace Kelly) also chose them for the bridesmaids' attire at her royal wedding.

Since 1993, Priscilla of Boston has been guided by Patricia Kaneb, who unstintingly adheres to the principles of her predecessor, with all gowns still handmade in Charlestown, Massachusetts. They currently offer five design collections—including veils of hand-rolled fabric—all designed to complement the type and style of wedding chosen by the bride-to-be.

Karen Stolman Parker and her husband Neil Parker. The wedding was on the heels of the Royal wedding of Diana and Charles, and brides were especially attracted to any detail that they might have seen, either via satellite or in newspapers or periodicals. (That royal affair, in fact, ushered in a period when "Trumpet Voluntary" frequently replaced the usual processional heralding of "Here Comes the Bride.") Just as Diana's gown was of fairytale proportions, Karen's gown, designed by her brother Steven Stolman, was also a big, fluffy confection. The two-piece gown had a tight-fitting bodice, ballgown skirt, and a fitted jacket with peplum, all in French tergal lace over tulle.

A FAMILY AFFAIR!

Fashion designer Steven Stolman (who has served for several years as the special events chairman of a well-known New York charity) played a major role in the weddings of his sisters, Karen and Stacey. Also prominently involved in Stacey Stolman's wedding were Jack Young, an advertising creative director who was responsible for the ceremony's elaborate program, and Richard Dalton, hairdresser to HRH Diana, Princess of Wales, who created hairstyling for the entire bridal party. The wedding was truly "a family affair."

Photography in this section by Cindy Lang Photography. Photographs courtesy of Stacey Stolman Webb and Dr. and Mrs. Joseph Stolman.

Stacey Stolman Webb in the bridal gown designed by Steven Stolman *(right)*. With its ivory guipure lace bodice, scoop neckline and short sleeves over a bouffant skirt in silk duchesse satin, the design complemented the statuesque height of the bride (5' 10") by featuring drama and volume without fussy frills. At left is Steven Stolman with his two sisters.

The bridal party. All attendants' gowns and dresses designed by Steven Stolman.

The junior bridesmaid and ring bearer make their entrance, followed by the flower girls, intently "sprinkling the petals." The dresses are of bottle green iridescent taffeta trimmed with ivory lace. Note the Black Watch bows on the flower baskets and the bottle green pillow that cradles the rings.

Mr. and Mrs. Michael Webb following the ceremony.

A close-up of the attendants' gowns, which featured black wool boucle twinsets over Black Watch plaid silk taffeta ballgown skirts. Since the bridesmaids differed in height and size, the concept of "formal separates" was quite effective . . . and had the added bonus of giving the attendants a black twinset to wear for many future occasions, both formal and informal. To complement the Black Watch plaid, groomsmen accented their traditional tuxedos with Black Watch plaid bow ties and cummerbunds.

Both professional chefs, the bride and groom planned and executed the bridal reception menu. This monumental wedding cake is the creation of Cheryl Kleinman Cakes, Brooklyn, New York.

An elegant fairyland awaits the reception guests.

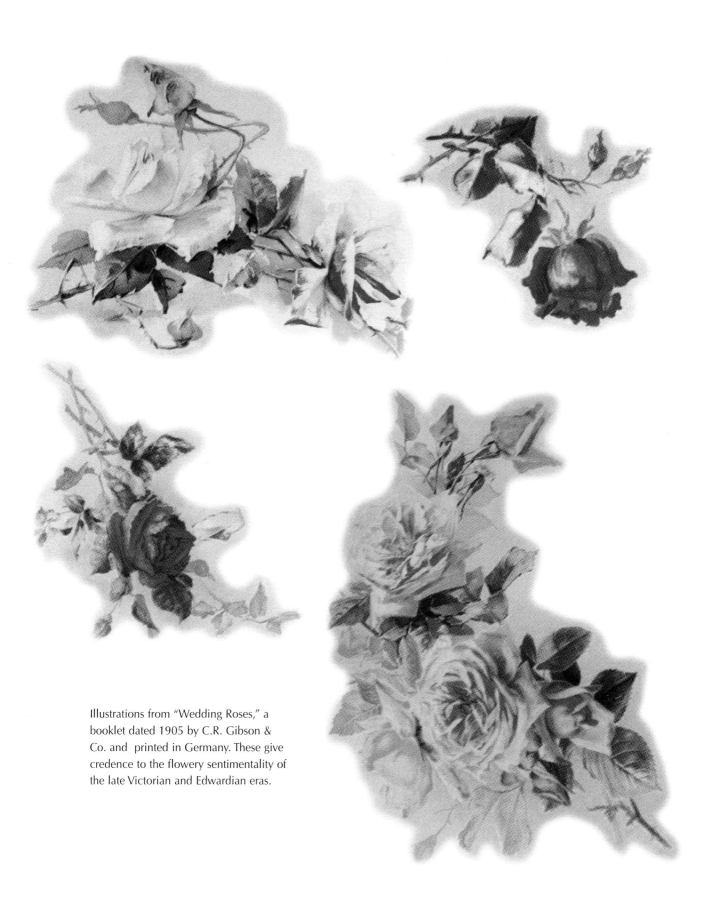

Illustrations from "Wedding Roses," a booklet dated 1905 by C.R. Gibson & Co. and printed in Germany. These give credence to the flowery sentimentality of the late Victorian and Edwardian eras.

# EPILOGUE

And from the window of a Charleston, S.C. antique shop, this piece of advise that served as a lasting gift from a Southern grandmother to her granddaughter:

"My dear, this is something you must always remember. Your bosom can be fake. Your smile can be fake. Your hair color can be fake. But your pearls and your silver must always be real."

*W*HERE TO FIND ITEMS SHOWN

VINTAGE CLOTHING AND ACCESSORIES

JANA STARR ANTIQUES
236 E. 80th Street
New York, NY 10021

ROBERTS ANTIQUES
Micanopy, FL

PERIOD BRIDAL THEME WEDDINGS

ROSE D'ZYNES
2479 S. Sante Fe
Vista, CA 92083

CURRENT BRIDAL GOWNS

BETSEY JOHNSON
Showroom Seven
498 Seventh Ave., 24th Floor
New York, NY 10018

PRISCILLA OF BOSTON
40 Chambridge Street
Charlestown, MA 02129

BRIDESMAIDS AND MOTHERS OF THE BRIDE AND GROOM (WITH A MODERN BENT)

STEVEN STOLMAN SOUTHAMPTON
38 Main Street
Southampton, NY 11968
and
311 Worth Avenue
Palm Beach, FL 33480

BRIDAL ACCESSORY DESIGNS

Barbra Music
246 W. 80th St., Studio 21
New York, NY 10024

FLORAL DESIGNS

Atlas Floral Decorators, Inc.
The Plaza
2 Central Park South
New York, NY 10019

WEDDING CONFECTIONS

Catherine Stebinger
171 B Main Street
Deep River, CT 06417

Cheryl Kleinman Cakes
Brooklyn, NY

ILLUSTRATIONS AND ORIGINAL ART WORK

Alan M. Goffman
American Illustration
264 E. 78th St.
New York, NY 10021

HISTORICAL ART

D. J. Neary, Artist
Heritage Studio
2852 Jeff Davis Highway
Suite 109-12
Stafford, VA 22554
(Note: "Till Death Us Do Part" available as limited edition print)

BRIDAL PARTY JEWELRY AND GIFTS

A Piece of the Rainbow
1015 Camelia Street
Berkeley, CA 94710

ECLECTIC SCULPTURE AND ART

Toby Buonaguerio
1723 Holland Avenue
Bronx, NY 10462

TO VIEW VINTAGE COSTUMES AND/OR AUTHENTIC DECOR

The Metropolitan Museum in New York, NY
The Smithsonian Institution, Washington, D.C.
The Fashion Institute, New York, NY
The Mark Twain House, Hartford, CT
Hill-Stead Museum, Farmington, CT
The Harriet Beecher Stowe House, Hartford, CT

A wealth of information on authentic period costumes and interiors also awaits you in the historical societies, museums, and photo libraries of most cities and states.

OTES

Notes for Chapter 1
1   Lacey, *The Wedding*, 104.
2   Wallenchinsky and Wallace, *The People's Almanac # 2*, 865.
3   *The Wedding*, 74.
4   ibid, p. 122.
5   *The People's Almanac #2*, 867.
6   *The Wedding*, 36.
7   *The People's Almanac #2*, 865.
8   Kuntz, *Rings for the Finger*, 194.
9   Ball and Torem, *Masterpieces of Costume Jewelry*, 33.
10 *Rings for the Finger*, 200.
11 *The Wedding*, 170.
12 *Rings for the Finger*, 205.
13 *The Wedding*, 26.
14 ibid, p. 78.
15 Hill-Stead Museum Archives

Notes for Chapter 2
1   *The Wedding*, 43.
2   *Rings for the Finger*, 205.
3   *The Wedding*, 179.
4   ibid, p. 110.
5   Tasman, *Wedding Album*, 11.
6   *The Wedding*, 60.
7   ibid, 132.
8   Cable, *American Manners and Morals*, 57.
9   *The Wedding*, 128-129.
10 *American Manners and Morals*, 37.
11 *The Wedding*, 170.

Notes for Chapter 3
1   *American Manners and Morals*, 167.
2   ibid, p. 167.
3   ibid, p. 170.
4   Hart, Grossman, and Dunhill, *A Victorian Scrapbook*, 121.
5   *The Wedding*, 150.
6   Hill-Stead Museum Archives
7   ibid.
8   Lindemeyer, ed., *Victoria Book of Days*, 131.
9   Clemens, Cyril B., ed., *Mark Twain Wit and Wisdom*, 146-147.
10 ibid, 147.
11 Clemens, Susy, *Papa, an Intimate Biography of Mark Twain*, 114.

12 Harriet Beecher Stowe Center
13 Stowe, *Life of Harriet Beecher Stowe*, 198.
14 Harriet Beecher Stowe Center
15 *The People's Almanac #2*, 788-789.
16 Watkins, *Jane Austen's Town and Country Style*, 28.
17 Hodge, *Only a Novel: The Double Life of Jane Austen*, 158.
18 Cecil, *A Portrait of Jane Austen*, 98.
19 ibid, 171.
20 ibid, 169, 170.
21 *Jane Austen's Town and Country Style*, 23.
22 *A Portrait of Jane Austen*, 98.
23 *Jane Austen's Town and Country Style*, 160.
24 ibid, 29.
25 *The Wedding*, 165.
26 *A Portrait of Jane Austen*, 158.
27 Lyndall, *Charlotte Bronte, A Passionate Life*, 35.
28 ibid, p. 307.
29 *Victoria Book of Days*, p. 64.
30 *Charlotte Bronte, A Passionate Life*, 316.
31 *The Wedding*, 148.
32 *Charlotte Bronte, A Passionate Life*, 145.
33 ibid, 82.

Notes for Chapter 4
1   Neville, *The Eight*, 259.
2   Ball and Torem, *The Art of Fashion Accessories*, 15.
3   DeWeese-Weken, "A Bridal Retrospective," *Arts & Antiques*, May 1995, 103.

Notes for Chapter 5
1   *The People's Almanac #2*, 57.
2   ibid, 858.
3   Churchill, *Remember When*, 43.
4   *The People's Almanac #2*, 864.
5   *American Manners and Morals*, 311.
6   *The People's Almanac #2*, 311.
7   ibid, p. 860.

Notes for Chapter 8
1   Mebane, *Collecting Brides' Baskets and Other Glass Fancies*, 17.
2   Longford, *Louisa, Lady in Waiting*, 39.
3   Hill-Stead Museum Archives

BIBLIOGRAPHY

Ayers, Alex, ed. *Wit and Wisdom of Mark Twain.* New York: Harper & Row, 1987.

Ball, Joanne Dubbs, and Dorothy Hehl Torem. *The Art of Fashion Accessories.* Atglen, Pennsylvania: Schiffer Publishing, 1993.

Ball, Joanne Dubbs, and Dorothy Hehl Torem. *Masterpieces of Costume Jewelry.* Atglen, Pennsylvania: Schiffer Publishing, 1996.

Betjeman, John, and Geoffrey Taylor. *English Love Poems.* London and Boston, Massachusetts: Faber and Faber, 1957.

Blayney, Molly Dolan. *Wedded Bliss.* New York: Abbeville, 1992.

Bronte, Charlotte. *Jane Eyre.* New York: Random House, 1943.

Cable, Mary. *American Manners and Morals.* New York: American Heritage Publishing Co., Inc., 1969.

Cecil, David. *A Portrait of Jane Austen.* New York: Hill and Wang, 1978.

Churchill, Allen. *Remember When.* New York: Golden Press, Inc. and Ridge Press, Inc., 1967.

Clemens, Cyril B., ed. *Mark Twain Wit and Wisdom.* New York: Frederick A. Stokes Company, 1935.

Clemens, Susy. *Papa, an Intimate Biography of Mark Twain.* Edited by Charles Neider. Garden City, New York: Doubleday & Company, Inc., 1985.

DeWeese-Weken, Joy. "A Bridal Retrospective." *Arts & Antiques,* May 1995.

Ficklen, Anne, ed. *The Hidden Mark Twain.* New York: Crown Publishers, Inc., 1984.

Girouard, Mark. *Life in the English Country House.* New Haven, Connecticut and London: Yale University Press, 1978.

Gordon, Lyndall. *Charlotte Bronte, A Passionate Life.* New York and London: W.W. Norton and Co., 1994.

Hart, Cynthia, John Grossman, and Priscilla Dunhill. *A Victorian Scrapbook.* New York: Workman Publishing, 1989.

Hedrick, Joan D. *Harriet Beecher Stowe: A Life.* New York: Oxford University Press, 1994.

Hill-Stead Museum (booklet). Farmington, Connecticut: Board of Trustees, Hill-Stead Museum, 1988.

Hodge, Jane Aiken. *Only a Novel: The Double Life of Jane Austen.* New York: Coward, McCann & Geoghegan, Inc., 1972.

Howard, Andrew R. *Covered Bridges of Massachusetts.* Unionville, Connecticut: The Village Press, 1978.

Kuntz, George Frederick. *Rings for the Finger.* New York: Dover Publications, Inc., 1973.

Lacey, Peter. *The Wedding.* New York: Ridge Press, Grosset & Dunlap, 1969.

Lindemeyer, Nancy, ed. *Victoria Book of Days.* New York: Hearst Books, 1989.

Longford, Elizabeth. *Louisa, Lady in Waiting.* New York: Mayflower Books, 1979.

Marshall Field & Company. *The Bride's Book.* Chicago, Illinois, 1937.

Mebane, John. *Collecting Brides' Baskets and Other Glass Fancies.* Des Moines, Iowa: Wallace-Homestead Book Company, 1976.

Neville, Katherine. *The Eight.* New York: Ballentine Books, 1988.

O'Neill, Helen. "Daughter's Wedding, Mother's Dream." *The Hartford Courant,* March 10, 1996.

Prochnow, Herbert V. *The Public Speaker's Treasure Chest.* New York and London: Harper & Brothers, 1942.

Peterson, William J. *Harriet Beecher Stowe Had a Husband.* Wheaton, Illinois: Tyndale House Publishers, 1983.

Shapiro, Ann. *Unlikely Heroines: Nineteenth-Century American Women Writers and the Woman Question.* Westport, Connecticut: Greenwood Press, 1987.

Stowe, Charles Edward. *Life of Harriet Beecher Stowe.* Boston and New York: Houghton, Mifflin and Company, 1889.

Tasman, Alice Lea Mast. *Wedding Album.* New York: Walker and Company, 1982.

Traub Manufacturing Company. *Wedding Ring Sentiment* (booklet). 1927.

Wallechinsky, David, and Irving Wallace. *People's Almanac #2.* New York: Bantam Books, Inc., 1978.

Watkins, Susan. *Jane Austen's Town and Country Style.* New York: Rizzoli, 1990.

About The Authors

A native of Lancaster, Pennsylvania and long-time resident of Connecticut, Joanne Dubbs Ball previously authored *"Costume Jewelers, the Golden Age of Design"* and *"Jewelry of the Stars, Creations from Joseff of Hollywood."*

A recent bride, Caroline Torem-Craig is a resident of both Rhode Island and New York City. Along with a career in jewelry design, she is a contributing photographer for New York's fashion magazine *Paper.*

In addition to *"Wedding Traditions—Here Comes the Bride,"* Ball and Torem-Craig also collaborated on *"Commercial Fragrance Bottles," "The Art of Fashion Accessories," "Masterpieces of Costume Jewelry,"* and *"Fragrance Bottle Masterpieces."*

BRIDAL NOTES:

BRIDAL NOTES:

 RIDAL NOTES:

BRIDAL NOTES: